IT'S ONLY A FEW PILLS!

~ and my life in pharmacy

PAUL RODGERS

Published by www.lulu.com

Copyright © Paul Rodgers, 2009

A CIP catalogue record for this book is available from the British Library.

ISBN 978-1-4092-9979-0

Please note:

The information given in some parts of my story, particularly covering the use of drugs and procedures, is subject to change. While I have made every effort to make sure details are accurate at the time of writing, do take care to ensure you get the latest facts by asking your local pharmacist.

The names of the pharmacies I worked in and the people I worked with during my career in pharmacy have been altered to preserve their privacy.

Paul Rodgers is a pen name

1

The manager's office was hot and very stuffy even though it was only just after nine o'clock in the morning. A large wooden desk took up most of the space in the room. Four trays labelled "In", "Out", "Maybe" and "No!" were arranged in a line at one end of it and each of them was heaped with paperwork. A tweed cap, a pair of tweezers and a glass jam jar holding several pencils, pens and a small plastic ruler sat upon the scarred surface along with two staplers, a tape measure, an apple and a mug of what looked like cold tea.

I inhaled a strong smell of herbal throat sweets. Shelves full of files and books covered one wall, an enormous ancient safe stood on the floor in the corner of the room, its door wide open, and an old fashioned adding machine without its paper roll completed the office equipment. Mr Johns leaned back in his seat and waved me toward the chair facing his own across the desk.

'Sit down,' he said.

A calender for 1968 was pinned to the wall behind his head showing a scene of a beautiful beach. People were throwing beach balls, flying kites or lying in deck chairs. The sun was shining and gulls flew among a few white puffy clouds. It looked lovely.

The name of the place, Whitesands Bay, was written across the bottom of the picture and I recalled a childhood holiday in Pembrokeshire. There had been thousands of seabirds on the offshore islands and we had seen seals and dolphins in the channel. I would have traded that hard seat for a place on that beach right there and then.

Notes and reminders were scribbled on or stuck to most of the days of that month and I noted the words "student newjoin" in red ink on the current day, Monday 5th August. 'That'll be me then,' I whispered to myself.

I twitched up the knees of my stiff new trousers and sat down. My tie felt tight around my neck and my armpits sweated under my jacket. Three years of student life, wandering around in T-shirts and jeans, loitering in pubs and day-dreaming about gap years were over. Life was getting serious now.

The old wooden chair creaked as I leaned forward slightly, the better to listen and learn from the wise words I anticipated would flow from my new boss. We hadn't met before this moment and, I realised, he would be checking me out too. Sit straight, don't slouch and look alert, I reminded myself.

Mr Johns was in his late fifties, short, chunky but not fat, his hair thinning but very carefully plastered across his head. Brylcream was still in fashion then in 1968, hair styling gels would follow much later. He wore a smart jacket of green and brown tweed, a white shirt and a tie patterned with vegetables. I could make out cabbages, beetroot and peas on it. There were two pens and the flat end of a small screwdriver showing in his breast pocket. Everything else was out of sight, below the level of the desk.

His hands were large and they looked capable of doing anything he found necessary but I noted a large bruise on the nail of his right thumb. Left-handed then, I thought. I've hit my thumb with a hammer and got a bruise just like that a few times as well. He looked fairly fit. Later I discovered he had been a keen rugby player in his youth. Inevitable I suppose, given his Welsh ancestry.

The eyes that looked back across the desk were a bright clear greeny-blue and his eyebrows were a sort of ginger colour and quite thick. They seemed to move independently of each other and of his facial expression. I was to spend most of the following year being distracted from his wise counsel by those meandering eyebrows.

The date marked on that calendar was 5th August 1968 and I had graduated from the University of Aston in Birmingham a few weeks before. Three years of blood, sweat and tears, as they say, were over but I had my Bachelor of Science degree in Pharmacy. My parents had been so proud of my achievement that they'd put the certificate in a neat frame and now it hung in the front room, the best room, of their house.

Now all I had to do was to successfully complete one year of post-graduate work (the pre-registration year they call it nowadays) under the supervision of another pharmacist before I could register with the Pharmaceutical Society of Great Britain and so begin my professional career. Mr Johns was the man chosen to supervise my efforts.

I never had an interview before starting that, my first job. During my last few months at university I had been contacted by the company. It was quite out of the blue. I had no idea how they selected my name and address although I found out much later that I was one of hundreds of students who were approached in the same way. I guess they found me through the pharmacy department at the university.

The company was offering new graduates the opportunity (as they put it) of taking advantage of their management training scheme during the required year of supervision. The starting salary offered was much less than that of a registered pharmacist but to them we were still students. They are just using us as cheap labour, I'd thought at the time, but I did need to start earning some money and agreed to join the company.

A letter arrived as soon as the company's head office was notified that I'd graduated. It informed me that I should start work at their Barnsgrove branch on the outskirts of Birmingham on the fifth day of August at 8.45 am. I was to report to the branch manager, a Mr W A Johns.

Walter Archibald Johns was the pharmacist who would be supervising my work for that next year and so it was important that I should prove to him that I was a suitable person to become a pharmacist. It would be vital to appear efficient, honest, capable of working to a high degree of accuracy, be healthy, be utterly reliable and, most difficult of all at that moment in that stuffy room, be wide awake. That degree and three years of hard work would count for nothing without his signature on my record of achievement at the end of the next twelve months.

*

An hour or so had passed by and I could feel my eyelids drooping. Mr Johns was still droning on. And on. The sun had moved around to shine directly through the window onto the back of my head. The room felt even hotter and more stuffy than before. He didn't ask me any questions and didn't appear to notice any of my comments but just rambled away with his account of how he saw the future of the company and what my own not inconsiderable part would play in its success. I gave up trying to join in a discussion or offer my comments and settled back to listen.

After a while, my mind drifted off into a daydream which involved the attractive young woman who had greeted me when I arrived. She had smiled as if she was really pleased to see me and then led the way through the dispensary into the staff area.

At the end of a drab corridor she showed me a stack of lockers and said to leave my things in one of them. I found an empty one, although none of them had locks that worked anyway, and then followed her along another corridor. I wondered why the whole place was painted brown and cream like a railway station.

She was about five foot seven or eight in height, I guessed, and I could make out a trim figure even beneath the standard company overall. I had already noted her friendly eyes, snub nose, cheerful grin and a bob of hair, brown and of medium length. Nice legs, pert bum, I thought to myself as I followed her up the stairs. Then she showed me into the office, introduced me to Mr Johns and disappeared. I hoped I might be working closely with her later, perhaps we could get to know one another better as the next twelve months went by.

'And I don't want any goings-on with the girls in the stockroom,' he was saying. I suddenly realised that I hadn't been listening for a while.

'Mmm?' I managed to say with a start before my new boss went on. Had I spoken my thoughts out loud?

'The last post-grad student we had here got too damned ... er ... friendly by half with some of my staff. I'm not having that!' His eyebrows shimmied across his forehead with emotion. 'He's gone now, thank heavens. You just watch out for those girls and stay out of trouble!'

I wanted to ask which girl. Surely not the nice one I had only just met. There must be other staff in the place. And what 'goings-on'? How many girls? Which ones should I watch out for? I stayed silent and listened more closely as the manager continued with his welcoming speech. At last he stood up and opened the door.

'Right! Well I've got things to do so you go back down to the dispensary and give Mrs Moore a hand until lunchtime. It'll take you a while to get used to our way of working I expect.' He paused to take a swig from the mug of cold tea on his desk and his face screwed up in disgust, although whether for the tea or me I wasn't sure. 'And I suppose it'll take a while for us to get used to you as well.'

*

That same young woman was working in the dispensary when I eventually found my way back there. She must have heard me coming and, having finished sticking a label onto a bottle of some mixture or other, turned round.

'I'm Paul,' I said and put my hand out to shake hers. 'Paul Rodgers. I'm to be working here for the next twelve months. Are you Mrs Moore?'

'Hell's teeth, no!' the same cheerful smile and a brisk, firm handshake. 'I'm Janet. Mrs Moore has just popped upstairs for a quick tea break. She won't be long. I don't think she trusts me working alone yet. I've only just finished the dispensing course so I'm still learning. Officially I'm called an improver. Whatever that means.

'Amy's the other dispenser here. We did the course together. Nearly drove the poor old dear over the edge. Mrs Moore I mean. She's very determined that we should be the best dispensers in the world. I think we might have been a little disappointing to her. She seemed to be aiming a bit higher than we had in mind. Amy's got a day off today so you'll see her tomorrow. Nice to meet you. You've had the welcome talk then?'

'I've just spent an hour or so listening to Mr Johns,' I said.

'Archie does go on a bit doesn't he,' she laughed and reached for the next prescription form. 'He's Welsh you see. They do like to talk don't they.'

'Archie?'

'That's just between us. The staff. When he's not in hearing distance,' she smiled. 'His hearing is excellent mind you, so be careful.'

'That's two warnings to be careful I've had so far and I haven't been here half a morning yet,' I grumbled.

'Two?' Her blue eyes looked up, puzzled.

'Mm yes. I'll ask about the other one later.'

Another woman, a lot older than Janet, came into the dispensary. I noticed her crisp white overall, almost shining in its whiteness like a saintly aura, and her business-like manner. She introduced herself; Mrs Moore. Even with my lack of experience I could see she exuded the air of a capable and efficient person.

Although the accepted hierarchy placed the pharmacist above a dispenser in terms of responsibility, in reality the good team recognises each other's knowledge and experience. I remembered one of our lecturers saying that. As a mere student, recently let out of university, I knew I wouldn't get anywhere trying to lord it over someone of Mrs Moore's age or ability. She would have worked with far more pharmacists than I had so far, and more experienced ones too. I resolved to listen and learn. I knew I would learn as much from her, Janet and the other staff as from Mr Johns himself.

'I've just seen Archie,' she said to Janet. 'He's busy upstairs, or so he says, so we're to carry on and check each other. We're to call him if anything awkward comes in.' The look on her face suggested that few, if any, problems would be beyond her capability.

'He did say he had lots of things to do,' I said.

'He's hiding,' Janet laughed and Mrs Moore sighed as she added quietly. 'Avoiding Betty, or Betty's customers more like.'

'Hiding?' I looked at them both as they nodded in unison.

'Betty is due to retire at the end of this week,' Janet explained in a whisper. 'She's been working here for about thirty-five years. She started long before Archie himself arrived.' She pointed to a stout woman in a white overall, standing just then at the far end of the counter. Betty turned to speak to a customer as Janet spoke and I noted a sour face, a thin lipped and downturned mouth, huge butterfly-wing glasses and a tight bun of grey hair. 'Her hearing's not too good these days but she doesn't miss much.'

'She started here even before I did!' Mrs Moore muttered. 'She's the last of the old staff who were here when the place opened.

'For all that time she has been ultra polite and always helpful to the customers. She looks a bit grim but everyone says she is a lovely person. Or so you would think,' Janet continued. 'But it seems that she's been keeping a little black book as well.'

'Little black book?' I was still puzzled.

'All the people who have ever been unpleasant or rude to her are listed in her book, she says. Now she is due to retire and she's taking her revenge in no uncertain terms. Most of our customers are quite pleasant, some of them have been coming here for years, but there are a few regulars who aren't very nice at all. Any of those who happen to come in this week and upset Betty are in for a shock.'

'Yes. We've had a couple of them already,' Mrs Moore took up the story. 'Betty's given them both barrels. It seems like the pressure has been building up all these years and she's finally blown. Archie doesn't want to be caught in the blast so he's been keeping out of sight. She finishes on Friday so he's hoping he won't have to do anything about her. He can't very well sack her now, not after all those years of service.'

'What if anyone complains to head office?' I asked.

'It would be a bit pointless after she's gone so I reckon Archie thinks it'll be easier to soothe them later than to try to tackle a volcanic Betty now.'

'There's your first lesson in management,' added Janet with a wide grin. 'And two warnings as well, you said. Not bad for your first morning.'

*

The dispensing workload increased as the morning went on. A never-ending queue of patients handed their prescriptions in or collected their medicines. The telephone rang more often than intermittently but not quite continuously and my head began to ache.

Working at university was hard at times and there had been some desperate moments during the exams but there was never this incessant level of noise and activity. I found it difficult to concentrate on checking the finished prescriptions while questions and interruptions flew at me from all sides.

'Phew!' I said when a slight lull came. 'Is it always this busy?'

'This isn't busy,' Mrs Moore stated firmly. 'This is what I call steady. You'll find life very different now you're out in the real world.'

As if to prove her point, an elderly couple approached the counter. It was just before my scheduled lunch break and I was certainly ready for a break by then. The man walked with a stick, his clothes looked shabby and his cap had a greasy sheen to it. His glasses were held together with several bands of black insulating tape. Wisps of smoke wafted up from his coat pocket as if a newly extinguished pipe had been stowed away in there.

His wife, as I presumed her to be, waddled and gasped asthmatically while carrying two bulging carrier bags a few paces behind him. A pink scarf clashed with her thick orange and green cardigan and her blue slacks were rolled up at the bottoms to display a pair of bright yellow socks stuffed into battered white sandals.

A circle of chairs was set out in the corner of the shop for the use of customers who waited for their prescriptions to be dispensed and the pair headed straight there. They settled down side by side with loud sighs and, as she dropped her bags on the floor, he looked up at me expectantly.

'Can I help?' I asked, leaning out across the counter and peering round the corner of the dispensary.

'I've got a sore foot,' the old man said and, with a struggle, lifted his right leg onto the chair opposite him. He pointed a grimy finger at his shoe. 'Have a look at it for me, lad.'

'It's a corn I reckon. Just wants a plaster on it.' his wife added helpfully with a saucy wink and a toothless smile at me.

'I'm sure we do sell corn plasters here, sir,' I said as I went over to them then I hesitated, unsure of myself already. 'I'm new here but we could take a look at your foot if you like. To make sure it really is a corn.' I looked round for support but both Janet and Mrs Moore had disappeared. A glance along the counter revealed that only Betty was available. I tried to catch her eye but she ignored my silent plea for help.

'I can't bend nowadays, my back's bad,' the old man said. 'You'll need to take the shoe off.'

I gingerly untied the laces on the grubby shoe and pulled it off his foot. An appalling stench filled my nostrils and my eyes started to water.

'I don't mind you taking me sock off,' the old man added helpfully.

A filthy foot appeared from within the sock and I dragged my eyes away from the sight of his black toenails to look at the grimy sole beneath.

'Yes, that'll be a corn,' I said through clenched teeth, trying not to breathe. 'Do you want to buy some corn plasters? I'll find them for you.'

I searched along the unfamiliar shelves to find some corn plasters then returned to see that neither of the pair had moved at all. His filthy bare foot still lay on the chair and his shoes and socks were on the floor beneath.

'Stick one on it for me lad,' the man seemed happy to sit there for ever. His wife was busy sorting out the contents of her bags. Out of the corner of my eye I saw that Betty had looked round at last, a faint smile flickered but just in the corners of her mouth.

I was a young, inexperienced but trying to do my best sort of chap and it didn't occur to me that this chap's wife could have applied the thing for him quite easily when they got home.

First I fetched some damp tissues and cleaned up the offending area as well as I could in the circumstances. Then I dried it and applied one of the plasters while trying not to actually touch the skin. I put the sock and shoe back on with a feeling of relief. The ordeal was almost over. Feeling faint, not least from lack of air caused by not breathing, I went into the dispensary to wash my hands.

A jolly good scrub later and I felt that the smell was beginning to fade at last. I took a couple of deep breaths but then remembered that I hadn't taken any money for those corn plasters and shot back out to the counter only to find that both of them had disappeared.

'They've gone without paying for those corn plasters,' I said to Betty, panic rising with my voice.

'Too late now,' she replied with an evil smirk. 'I'm off for my lunch break. All yours.'

Of course I confessed my mistake when Mrs Moore returned to the dispensary. I even offered to pay for the plasters myself but she shook her head.

'We know them,' she said. 'They'll be back in. We'll remind them they haven't paid. I don't think they would steal anything. I expect they just forgot about it. You must have dazzled them with your talent. I must admit I wouldn't go near his foot with a barge pole.'

*

Closing time arrived at last. Archie came warily down the stairs into the dispensary and checked the time. There were no more customers in the pharmacy and Betty had already gone up to get her bag and jacket.

'I make it six o'clock,' he said looking relieved that another day was over. He wasn't alone in that. I felt exhausted. We locked the cupboards, tidied away the tablet counters and medicine measures, put the takings in the safe and fetched our belongings from the lockers in the corridor.

'Quite an eventful day,' I said as we closed the shop door behind us.

'And they won't get any easier,' Janet swung her bag up onto her shoulder, 'See you tomorrow!'

2

I was born and bred in Worcestershire and spent my childhood around the hamlet of Ipsley, climbing trees, making dens in the woods and occasionally falling into the river Arrow which meanders through the nearby meadows. The whole area is now part of the new town of Redditch and much of the building development took place during the years I was studying at university.

The new town and its roads and industrial estates soon surrounded, indeed smothered, my favourite haunts. Remnants of my woods and meadows do remain and some of my family still live in the area but I don't think of the place as home now.

That first job, in Barnsgrove on the edge of Birmingham, was about ten miles from my parent's house and to begin with I commuted each day in my old grey Austin A35 van. Soon after I started work there I began to look around for a flat of my own. I searched through the adverts in the local papers, spent hours peering at notice boards in shop windows and also asked the staff at the shop to look out for anything suitable.

It was Betty of all people who came up with one of the first suggestions. She had retired by then but came into town each week to do her shopping. Almost without fail she also came into the pharmacy to pick up any gossip. One good thing was that she had at least cheered up a lot since her retirement. Sometimes she seemed almost warm and friendly.

'There's a room to let in one of the houses in my road,' she informed me one day. 'It would be just right for you.'

'Oh I see. Thank you but I'd been thinking in terms of getting a flat,' I replied. 'So that I can come and go as I want. If I'm just a lodger I'll have to fit into their ways, eat at their meal times and so on.'

'You can't be too fussy,' she went on. 'There aren't many flats around here at a reasonable rent. You should at least have a look at it. I'll tell Mrs Davies you're coming tonight, straight after work. The house is called "Malvern View". You'll find it easy enough, its got a green fence and a blue front door.'

Betty had been talking at me as I tried to work and it was only after she had gone that I realised that I didn't know where she lived. Fortunately, Janet did know and drew me a sketch map during a quiet moment just before we finished work.

'Betty lives in one of the bungalows at the bottom end of that road,' she traced her finger over the map. 'She said this "Malvern View" is a house didn't she so I reckon it'll be up the hill, at the other end of the road. About there,' She paused. 'I bet it hasn't got a view of the Malvern Hills though. Not from there.'

*

I found the house just where Janet had suggested it might be. It was a large gloomy looking place in need of some maintenance. In fact it was on the verge of becoming a derelict mess. I drove up to the front gate.

The house had probably once been an elegant home, a successful businessman's abode perhaps. It had been nicely set in a spacious plot but now the garden had turned into an overgrown jungle. Only a few rose bushes in need of severe pruning and two ancient plum trees stood clear of the tangles of weeds.

A narrow path made of broken concrete slabs took me up to the front door. I knocked and then turned to inspect the view while I waited for an answer. Janet had been right, there was no chance of seeing anywhere as attractive as the Malvern Hills from that spot. What may have once been a lovely view across open countryside now overlooked yet another industrial estate and its attendant warehouses, roads and car parks.

Mrs Davies opened the door at last. It had once upon a time been painted light blue but was now peeling badly. She was in a similar condition, a weary-looking fifty-something in a drab grey cardigan, brown trousers and slippers that looked as though they had been made from a beige carpet. She invited me inside.

A widow now, she explained as we walked through the house, and she had lived there for twenty-four years. Her youngest daughter, Rosemary, was there as well. She was twenty-two years old. The daughter was reading a book in her bedroom when Mrs Davies led me through to show me the room that was available to rent.

'Um, do I have to come through your daughter's bedroom to get to this room?' I asked.

'Oh yes, this is the only way in. She won't mind,' Mrs Davies went on to demonstrate how the cupboard doors opened and pointed out a chest of drawers and even a bookshelf. The bed would have been a tight fit for a twelve year old and the mattress sagged all over the place. She looked round with a smile as if satisfied that the room would be irresistible to me. 'It will be five pounds a week for the room,' she said. 'Then we'll have to come to an arrangement about meals and so on.'

I glanced back through the door at the young woman who was lying on the bed and still reading. She hadn't moved as we'd walked through. The book was lowered slightly and a long, mean face topped with a stiff mop of heavily bleached hair came into view. Her thin lips were clamped over clenched teeth. Her nostrils flared and a look of sheer loathing blazed from her bleak eyes like a death ray in a science fiction story, then the book was raised again.

'Blimey!' I muttered under my breath. 'Fancy meeting that every morning.'

'We could also come to some arrangement if you would be able to help out around the place. Perhaps in the garden?' Mrs Davies had carried on with her sales pitch. I wasn't listening. I was thinking of excuses to leave.

Mercifully Amy, the other dispenser at work, came up with a better idea the next morning. I went to have a look at it during my lunch break. It was a small flat over a nearby hairdresser's salon which would be vacant at the end of the month.

Two cheerful girls from the salon showed me round and didn't seem to notice the sickly smell of hair dyes, bleach and perm that suffused the building. 'I suppose you get used to it after a while,' one of them said when I mentioned it.

There was one large room with an area partitioned off to provide a space for the bed. It all looked quite modern and freshly decorated and although I'd have to pay for the gas used for cooking and a heater, all the electricity was included.

'What you'll use up here is a drop in the ocean to what we use downstairs in the salon,' one of the girls said. 'Our boss said it wouldn't be worth trying to work it out.'

The rent would be five pounds a week and for that I had my own entrance, a neat kitchenette and a nice bathroom. I soon got used to the smell of the toiletries. It was perfect.

*

Amy had just completed the same dispensing course as Janet. I met her on my second morning and was immediately struck by their different attitudes to the job. Janet was a very careful, efficient, worker. I had swiftly decided that she would turn out to be a new Mrs Moore when she had more experience. She had just the right sort of attitude for the work and her customers loved her.

On the other hand, everything that Amy did had to be checked carefully. She was prone to making errors, especially with medicines having similar names, and there are a great many of those. I think her mind was permanently elsewhere. This is a dangerous state to be in while dispensing and I soon got into the habit of checking her work very carefully indeed.

She was a tall girl, almost my height, about twenty years old, with long, lank, mousy brown hair cut with what was a fashionable fringe of the time. Straight across the eyebrows. Amy embraced any new fad or fashion with enthusiasm. A new lurid shade of lipstick or an even blacker black mascara sent her into ecstasy.

The 1960s had brought us new music, miniskirts, lipsticks in every colour and thick black eye shadow. Panda eyes we called them. Amy had panda eyes in spite of the company's rules about staff appearance. And the shortest skirts in town. I was to find that she also seemed to have embraced the 1960's ideas of sexual freedom.

As a fairly shy, well brought up lad, I was unbelievably naive when I started work. I managed to go through university during the 1960s without discovering sex, drugs or rock'n'roll. The music of Peter, Paul and Mary was more to my taste. Studying too hard is my only excuse for such a gentle lifestyle.

Also I lived at home and travelled into Birmingham each day while at university so I missed the life in student halls of residence that many of my eager contemporaries discovered to be such a free and easy one.

By far the greatest majority of people who work in pharmacies are female. These days there are more female than male pharmacists too. We male pharmacists are becoming an endangered species. Girls and women of all ages, especially when in groups, scare me. They did in 1968 and to some extent they still do. They are unpredictable, more self-aware and often a lot tougher than men, and they don't like young male managers giving them orders.

*

I had been working at Barnsgrove for a couple of weeks before I discovered that the pharmacy had a cellar. The practice of pharmacy was changing fast by the time I came into the profession. Most of the medicines we dispensed then came as stock jars of tablets and capsules from which we counted out the numbers required or in large glass bottles called winchesters filled with various mixtures.

We no longer made pills. In fact we made up only a few items of any sort, mostly cough mixtures or stomach medicines or ointments. Many of the recipes were traditional ones listed in the British National Formulary. Some old favourites such as the cough mixtures, Mist. Tussi Nig. and Mist. Expect, were made in bulk in the pharmacy but most of our stock arrived ready made.

Once in a while a prescription arrived for something that just had to be made as a one-off. Such a prescription for an ointment which had probably last been used regularly during the First World War turned up one Friday afternoon. The elderly doctor had even written it out with the quantities in grains, fluid ounces and drachms. Dispensing had gone metric, moved into milligrams and millilitres, by the 1960s so I had to convert the formula into metric units. As I did so I thought to ask if we'd still have the necessary ingredients in stock.

'Probably down in the cellar,' Mrs Moore said without looking up from her work. 'You'll have to go and see what's there.'

'Cellar?' I asked. 'Where's that?' She turned and looked at me as if I was an idiot.

'Can you show him, Amy,' she growled at last. 'And don't be long about it.'

Amy smiled at me and fluttered her panda eyes. We went out into the stockroom and Amy opened a brown and cream painted wooden door I hadn't noticed before. Probably because it matched the brown and cream paint on the wall. Steep wooden steps disappeared down into the darkness.

Amy flicked a switch and we went down into a dimly lit, dusty room. There was barely head room for either of us as we began our search for those ingredients. In the old days the cellar had been used for storage and when making up the gallons of mixtures and lotions used in the dispensary above. Later I found out that the huge marble slab had been used when making large quantities of ointments and what I took to be a witch's cauldron was used for mixing some of the animal medicines they used to supply in bulk to the local farmers.

Along one wall were rows of shelves holding a variety of boxes, jars and bottles. A stack of thick prescription books like old Dickensian ledgers were piled at one end. All of them were thick with dust. I brushed the dirt off one jar and found a lovely old label written in copperplate hand and apparently in Latin.

'What on earth is P:PECTORAL?' I asked. Amy shrugged. I took the top off and peered inside but there was just a solid lump of something nasty-looking in the bottom of the jar.

'The stuff you want for that old ointment might be along there,' she said and, not wanting to get herself covered in cobwebs, pushed me into the far corner of the room.

I had to wipe away a lot of dust and spiders webs before eventually finding the items I needed. Nowadays I would want to know at least what the expiry date was before I used any of those chemicals but then we just used what we had.

In fact nowadays we wouldn't stock any of those ingredients anyway. Any unusual or non-licensed medicine would be ordered from one of the 'specials' manufacturers. All those old jars and chemicals were thrown out years ago. Although many pharmacies still have ointment slabs and dispensing balances, few use them now.

I placed the jars and bottles I needed on the bench and then backed out of the corner trying to brush the dust off my hands. Amy was close by, leaning seductively against the old marble slab. Her green eyes appeared half open from beneath her fringe and they sparkled under the bare lightbulb.

'There's not much room in here, cosy isn't it' she whispered and moved closer.

'Er, we'd better get back upstairs. Mrs Moore said not to be long. They're busy up there I expect.'

'Don't be a spoilsport,' she moved off the slab, pulled my arm round her waist and eased herself into my chest. I felt her right knee pushing against my left then the front of her thighs pressed on mine. It was a pleasant sensation, but I could hear Archie's warning words echoing in my ear. Her lips tasted warm and soft and lipsticky. The cellar began to feel hot and claustrophobic.

'Is there anyone down there?' It was Archie himself! Amy jumped back and put her finger to her lips. I gasped then found my voice.

'Yes, only me. I've just been getting something for a prescription, Just coming up now.'

'Oh, right. I couldn't hear anybody moving about down there so I thought some clot had left the light on. Have you found what you need?' A step sounded on the stairs. He must have been thinking of coming down to help my search. Amy's eyes opened wide in panic. It was as good an impression of a startled panda who had just stepped on a sharp bit of bamboo as you could wish for.

'Yes thanks. I'm just wiping the dust off and I'll be back in a minute.' I tried to sound casual.

We waited until he'd walked away, his footsteps sounding over our heads and fading, then we went back up into the dispensary.

'Sorry I was so long,' I said. 'The stuff was right in the corner, covered in dust. I'll carry on checking the formula.'

'That cellar's a terrible dump,' Mrs Moore said, then added. 'I'm thinking of having a good sort out down there now we've got you here. Another pair of hands, like. Most of the stuff should have been thrown out years ago.'

Amy went back to her work and Janet turned round to ask me to check her prescription as the patient was waiting. As she did so, her voice stalled. I watched her eyes linger on the dusty handprint on the back of Amy's white overall then look up into mine. Her lips pursed, her brow furrowed, she sighed.

'If you've got time,' she said.

*

I don't really know why it should be so, but I felt I had to apologize to Janet about that dusty patch on Amy's back. We were alone in the dispensary later so I tried to explain.

'I know what Amy is like,' she interrupted. 'She chases any man who ever comes in here. You just watch her the next time one of the drug company representatives call. Specially if he's a young bloke. Embarrassing, that's what it is.'

'She's really not my type,' I muttered.

'Have you heard about Amy and the student pharmacist we had here last year?' I shook my head, thinking about what Archie had said on my first day. 'No? Well I might as well tell you. Sooner or later someone will.' Janet looked out into the shop. The other girls were some distance away down the counter and no-one seemed to be waiting to be served.

'Gary was his name. He was what you might call a bit of a lad and went out with several different girls during his year here. Amy took a big shine to him but I think he just played her along for what he could get out of it. If you see what I mean.

'Anyway, Amy's mum and dad went away on holiday for a fortnight last Easter and Gary stayed at their house with her. They used to come in to work late every day, giggling and ignoring the rest of us. Heaven only knows what went on whenever they were alone anywhere in the building. Archie went mad when he walked into the stockroom one day and found them at it in there. They calmed down a bit after that but it was almost impossible to get any work out of either of them.

'Then there was a bust-up. Tears, shouting, threats, we had it all. We think she wanted him to stay with her, get married and all that. But his year here had just about finished and he was set on moving away to another area. He went up north somewhere I think. He was just using her. Not a nice young man.'

'So that's what Archie was warning me about the first day,' I said. 'That other warning I told you about. Well, now I know what he meant and I'm certainly not going into the cellar with her again.' Janet smiled at last. 'I hope you don't think I'm like that. She's not my type, honestly.'

'Good.'

3

The course I'd taken at university had left me with a head full of facts and figures, theories and ideas but the actual practice of pharmacy in the real world is a very different thing.

In such a well organised pharmacy as the one at Barnsgrove most of the actual dispensing was carried out by the dispensers. My job was to check the prescriptions for any likely prescribing errors or interactions, make a final check to ensure that the medicines had been dispensed with accuracy and to try to advise the patient of anything they needed to know about actually taking or using their medication.

By the way, using that phrase, 'dispensed with accuracy', can cause confusion. Years ago I remember seeing a showcard in a pharmacy window which read, 'We dispense with accuracy' and wondered whether they took every care with dispensed medicines or if they did away with, or managed without, accuracy when supplying medicines. Hopefully their customers weren't as pedantic as I am.

I certainly wasn't prepared for the work rate nor the huge responsibility placed on our young shoulders so soon. The most difficult thing of all I found was having to deal with the patients. I was completely unprepared for the attitude that the general public has to pharmacy. They seem to trust us most of the time but they simply don't really know what we do or why we have to do what we do in the way that we do it. Why should they, you might ask, and I would have to agree that we as a profession have never promoted ourselves properly.

People know, at least they think they do, what doctors and dentists do for them. They read novels about vets and policemen. They watch films, documentaries and television dramas about nurses and paramedics, firemen and soldiers, antique dealers, chefs, gardeners, fashionistas and estate agents.

Those people are usually portrayed as very popular and often as sympathetic characters. When, I might ask, did you last see a play, read a novel or even follow a soap opera that featured a pharmacist or was set in a pharmacy. Never? I thought as much.

I once spent a few hours searching for any reference to a pharmacist or pharmacy in films. There were three examples, just three, as far as I could tell. All of the films had been made over fifty years ago and none gave us a positive image.

A film called 'Pink String and Sealing Wax' was made in 1945 and starred Googie Withers and Gordon Jackson. The latter played a pharmacist who was persuaded to supply the poison to murder his lover's husband.

'In Old California', one of the western genre, was made in 1942. In it John Wayne took the part of a pharmacist. Actually he might have made a better job of the part than most as his father really was a pharmacist. Not many people know that.

Even earlier, in 1933, W C Fields featured in the film 'The Pharmacist'. It was said at the time that he portrayed "a hard-working, hen-pecked pharmacist with a termagant spouse, dysfunctional family and demanding clientele". I love the word termagant. He survived by imbibing frequent martinis and managed to keep his precarious business profitable by selling bootleg liquor under the counter to the growing suspicion of the local sheriff.

A poisoner, a cowboy and W C Fields as pharmacists. What role models! This is how pharmacy has been portrayed to the world. No wonder the great British public don't understand pharmacists.

I soon discovered that patients and customers treat the pharmacy staff in a variety of ways. Some just hurl abuse at anyone in sight and by and large we just have to put up with it. We comfort ourselves by saying that they should remember that no-one is going to put themselves out for them in the future if they abuse us.

On the other hand a worried parent with a sick child to deal with isn't going to be pleased if they have to wait for their medication. Even though sometimes it is not possible to dispense the item because of a query. If I had a pound for every time I've taken abuse in one ear while holding a telephone to the other and trying to get the doctor to clarify an ambiguous or downright wrongly written prescription, I'd have a Rolls Royce parked outside the front door. And possibly another one round the back of the pharmacy as well.

We also get very pleasant people who treat us with respect. Once in a while someone brings a thank you card or a gift for the help they've been given. Often just a little extra help brings a huge reward.

Late one Saturday afternoon, just before closing time, I answered the telephone to a man who sounded worried. He and his wife had just returned from a holiday and he'd had to call the duty doctor out because his wife felt ill. The man asked when we closed as he had a prescription to be dispensed. I said we closed at six o'clock, a matter of about ten minutes away.

'I can be there in about twenty minutes if you can wait,' he said. 'The doctor did say it was urgent, some antibiotics I think.'

'Come on in,' I said with an inward groan. 'It takes a while to close everything up anyway but we'll wait a few minutes. If the door is locked, knock hard and I'll come and let you in.'

As it happened he arrived only a few minutes after our usual closing time and it was no trouble to dispense his prescription and then let him back out of the shop. I doubt if we were more than ten minutes late leaving work that day. He was very pleased and grateful to receive his wife's medication and shook my hand firmly as he went.

Just before lunchtime on Monday he came back. On his shoulder he had a sack of potatoes and on his face, a broad grin.

'These are for you,' he said, 'Thank you again. My wife is much better today.'

It turned out that he was a local farmer and not only did I gain a sack of spuds but an acquaintance who was to help me out in the future.

*

In my innocence and through having a lack of real knowledge about the practice of pharmacy, I hadn't really considered what happened to the medicines after we'd supplied them. We go to great lengths to make sure the labels and instructions are clear, nowadays there are often leaflets as well, and we try to offer any advice we can to ensure the medicine is taken effectively. Then people pick up their medication, walk out of the pharmacy and disappear.

Some patients just don't read the labels or instruction leaflets or listen to what we say. Just thinking about the day that one lady walked slowly and carefully up to the counter still makes my eyes water. She came to complain that we had supplied her with some medication that had caused her untold damage and pain. I asked her what she meant.

She looked round to make sure we were alone then showed me a pack of suppositories which were used to help relieve constipation. She opened the box and took one of them out then thrust the thing up close to my face. I didn't see how they could have caused her any trouble.

'It's the sharp edges on that foil,' she whispered, her face reddening at the memory. 'They cut me. I was bleeding. It hurt. You shouldn't give out things like that.'

Apparently she had inserted the suppository without removing it from the foil wrapping. I gently explained her error. She just glared at me and then without another word she slowly and carefully stalked away.

We started adding the words 'Remove the foil wrapping first then...' in underlined capital letters to our labels before the instruction to 'insert the suppository...' from then on. Do please read the label and ask if you're not sure.

It had not occurred to me that so much of the medicine prescribed and dispensed would never actually be taken or used. One way that this manifests itself is in the amount of stock we get back whenever a patient clears out their store of medicines at home.

Often this happens when someone dies and a relative has to carry out the sad task of clearing their home. Invariably some medicines are found and hopefully they will be disposed of safely. For everyone's sake medicines mustn't be just dumped in bins or flushed down the toilet. The simplest and best way is to bring them to the nearest pharmacy. We have proper facilities nowadays to dispose of such items safely. It is an important part of our job.

I've often wondered why some patients hoard their medication. They order their repeat prescription regularly each month but for some reason never take the medicine even though their doctor had prescribed it for them. They don't seem to bother to tell the doctor that they are not taking the stuff but just put it in the cupboard with all the other boxes and bottles and re-order the same items again next month.

I have seen a whole year's supply returned in a bag with a sequence of twelve packs of the same medicine prescribed and dispensed at monthly intervals and none opened. What a waste! These medicines cost the Health Service, that is the taxpayer, a lot of money and even if returned unopened cannot be re-issued. It all has to be destroyed.

We, not to mention the medicine manufacturers, go to a lot of trouble to dispense medicines into suitable containers. These days many of our tablets and capsules are packed in foil strips, often with the days of the week printed on them to help patients remember to take their medication that day and to know they have already taken that day's dose if the think about it later. However, many people just pop their pills out of the foil randomly which makes the whole exercise a bit pointless.

I have often come across patients who tip all their medicines out of our bottles and cartons to store them in their own idea of a container. Once in a while someone will bring us a tupperware or similar box with several different tablets inside to ask us to identify what they are as they have forgotten what they are taking or for what condition. If they left the things in the original pack and read the leaflet that usually goes with it, they wouldn't have to ask.

On one afternoon in Barnsgrove a shoe box appeared on the dispensary counter. Clarkes shoes, apparently, mens dark brown tan size 9 it said on the label. I asked why it was there. The woman who had brought the box in to show me picked it up again and shook it. It rattled and when she removed the lid a small cloud of white dust fell out to settle on the counter. I took the box from her and looked inside. It was almost full of tablets. All loose and mostly white.

Now many tablets have a mark of some sort on them and if you have the time and patience you can sometimes find out what they are. However even now and it was certainly so forty years ago there were a lot of small tablets, often white, without an identifying logo or mark.

It can be very difficult to differentiate between one small white tablet and another. I tried to sort out some of the contents of the box. There were a few brightly coloured capsules and tablets which I could separate from the mass and give a name to.

Along with them and all mixed up together there were I would guess more than a couple of thousand tablets in that box. They were of at least twelve different kinds. Probably more than that. I was eventually able to recognise one or two of them but I could not put a name to most of them.

The woman told me that her mother had always stored her tablets in that manner but had become very ill. She had been in and out of the doctor's surgery several times just lately but no-one appeared to know what was wrong.

She was taking some tablets regularly, her daughter said, but which ones she didn't know. It seemed possible to me that judging by the shambles in the shoe box she might have been taking the wrong dose or even the wrong combination of medicines. There may even have been something in there that her doctor had prescribed in the past but had later told her to stop taking.

Then I discovered that it was also likely, according to her daughter, that she had kept some of her husband's tablets after he died and stored them in her box as well. In case they might come in useful in future!

I could picture her opening the box whenever she felt like taking a dose of medication and having what was in effect a lucky dip. I could see her taking out one of these and one of those and, perhaps today, a pink capsule at random and hoping for the best, if indeed she ever thought about it at all.

I suggested to the daughter that the best solution was to see the her mother's doctor to get new prescriptions for the correct medication and start again. Later she came back with a new prescription for just three items. They were the only types of tablets her mother should have been taking. Hopefully she now keeps them safely in the containers she was given and follows the instructions properly. We kept and later destroyed the collection of old tablets.

*

A teenage girl came into the pharmacy and handed two carrier bags full of unwanted medicines to me. A brief glance into the bags suggested that they contained some prescription drugs and a lot of over-the-counter branded medicines. I could see bottles of tablets, tubes of cream, some boxes of suppositories, a few bandages and plasters and bottles of various mixtures. It was a real mix of stuff out of someone's medicine cupboard.

'My granddad died,' she said. 'Mum asked me to give you all these things. Can you get rid of them for her please?'

'Yes,' I said. 'No problem. Leave it to us.'

We were very busy at the time so I left the two bags under the workbench at the back of the dispensary until we had chance to sort through the contents. It was Saturday afternoon before I remembered them so, as it was quiet in the dispensary, Janet and I started the job of sorting out what was there.

Most of the stock was easily dealt with. In those days, forty years ago, we flushed small amounts of tablets and capsules down the toilet. Nowadays everything has to be packed into an appropriate container and sent away, usually to be incinerated.

In the bottom of one bag, Janet found a small square but strong cardboard box. It was more of a cube shape really and rattled loudly when she shook it. There was no label on the box at all. She held the box out to show me.

'It doesn't sound like there are tablets in there unless its one very big one,' I said. 'Take the lid off and see what it is.'

Janet carefully lifted the top off the box and looked in. A penetrating scream echoed around the shop. Several customers and all the staff turned to stare. Janet flicked the box away from herself in a panic. Her frenzied action sent the contents of the box shooting across the dispensary. A spherical object narrowly missed my left ear, bounced on the shelf behind me then off the workbench itself. I grabbed what looked like a small ball as it passed my head again.

'Howzat!,' I shouted in triumph.

Opening my fingers revealed a clear brown eye staring up at me. I jumped in shock but managed to resist the impulse to throw the thing away as Janet had done when it stared up at her from within the box. I looked at it more closely.

'Its a false eye!' I exclaimed. 'Look' I reached over to show it to Janet. Her face went white then it went green. I had never seen a green complexion before. It was quite fascinating. She clapped her hand across her mouth and ran out of the dispensary. Some time later she returned.

'What have you done with that thing?' she demanded.

'I put it back in the box,' I replied with a sadistic grin. 'We can show it to the others on Monday.'

*

It was my turn to go green a few days later. One of our regular customers, a Mrs Mole, brought a large paper bag full of cakes and bread rolls in for us. One of the girls had delivered some urgently required medicine to her home a few days previously and she wanted to say thank you. She had been baking, she told us, and hoped we would enjoy them.

The cakes and rolls looked delicious as they were arranged on a plate and placed in the centre of the table in the staff room. There were enough for us to have a couple of them each plus some spares and Archie told us to help ourselves when we had our tea breaks.

At teatime someone went out to fetch some butter and cheese and we filled some of the rolls and settled down to enjoy them. I had a cake and one of the rolls and they really were lovely. I had almost finished a cheese roll when Amy came into the staff room and sat down.

'Have a bun or a cake,' I said. 'They're very nice.'

'No thanks,' Amy looked at the plate and shook her head, then she made a face.

'Oh go on, have one,' I said. 'These rolls really are delicious. There's some sort of seeds in them I think, chewy like.'

'No I don't want one,' she repeated firmly then went on to explain. 'I know that Mrs Mole. She lives next door to my Auntie Marge. I used to go round there and play with Mrs Mole's daughter, Jennifer, whenever I visited my Auntie,' she paused and flicked her hair back behind her ear. Her eyes disappeared behind her fringe as she screwed up her face again. 'Auntie Marge told me never, ever, to have anything to eat when I was round at Mrs Mole's house.'

'Why's that?' I asked when I'd swallowed the last piece of my bread roll.

'Well, she said that one day Mrs Mole told her that she reckoned making bread, kneading the dough like, was good for cleaning her nails.' I gulped. 'So I don't think I'll have one of those now, thank you.' She opened her magazine and started reading.

*

We had some nice customers, nasty customers, grateful patients and some who just grabbed their medication and ignored us. We also had embarrassed customers. Sometimes it was a query about a bodily function such as constipation or vaginal thrush.

At that time, in the 1960's, many people were still shy of asking for contraceptives. Often they used phrases like "a pack of three" or even "something for the weekend" to mean they wanted to buy a pack of condoms.

These days such items are out on open display but then we weren't allowed to display them at all. Condoms had to be kept in a drawer, out of sight, presumably in case the very sight of them corrupted an innocent passer-by. The customer had to actually approach the counter and ask for the things. Many people found that incredibly difficult to do, especially those young men who found that they had to ask an attractive young woman for their requirements.

The girls on the counter were quite unconcerned, even blasé, about their embarrassment but many men waited until Archie or I was available to serve them. They would indicate that they wanted a quiet word and we knew what they wanted straightaway as their requests were usually whispered and accompanied by a red face.

At Barnsgrove the condoms were stored in a drawer under the counter. There were only a few makes available at the time, nothing like the wide range one sees today. In an attempt to prevent even more embarrassment for our customers we put each pack of condoms inside a small plain paper bag before placing them into the drawer so that when we sold them we simply handed over something already wrapped that couldn't be seen for what it was. As the drawer was right under one of the tills however there were usually several witnesses to the sale anyway.

Putting the packs of condoms into the plain bags was one of those odd jobs for a quiet moment and, one afternoon, someone did just that. They carefully put one pack of condoms in each bag and then equally carefully stapled each bag shut so that there was absolutely no risk of a pack of condoms falling out of its bag as it was handed over to the customer. Therefore there would be a minimum amount of embarrassment for the customer. A great idea, she probably thought at the time.

And it was, until we discovered that the same someone had stapled through the condoms inside the pack as well as the paper bag. Condoms with holes in aren't much good, not fit for purpose as we'd say now. Several irate, red-faced customers returned their packs after that weekend and we reminded everybody to always use sellotape to seal the bags after filling them.

Later we had a problem with a product called C-film. This was a new type of contraceptive. It was a small square of clear film impregnated with a spermicide which had to be positioned over the penis rather like a small condom.

We had a new girl working with us at the time who was just finding her feet around the shop. She had only worked for the company for a short while but had already helped on the various departments; cosmetics, baby products, photographic and so on. She was coming along nicely but sometimes took a step too far in her product knowledge.

When a man asked for C-film one day she felt she could help by using her newly won experience. The problem was that she had never heard of C-film but had helped out on the photographic counter. None of us, especially the customer, knew what to say when she smiled sweetly and asked him to clarify his request.

'C-film?' she said. 'Yes of course. How many exposures would you like?'

4

Life certainly didn't get any easier. I soon learned about the sheer variety of tasks to be performed and, being the new boy, I had to do them all. At least I had to attempt them. Apart from the never-ending stream of prescriptions to be dispensed and questions to answer, we had to order all of the stock we needed, check off deliveries, chase up discrepancies, then clean and maintain the dispensary and deal with the paperwork. Oh the paperwork! That was before I learned anything about managing the branch.

Even something as simple-sounding as cashing up the tills was fraught with problems. At first nothing balanced, change seemed to vanish into thin air only to re-appear somewhere else later and the company's accounting systems were unfathomable.

It could take me half a day just to put up the wages. This was before the days of computers or even calculators in general use so everything was added up and recorded with pen and paper.

Then I had to learn how to take on all the other roles expected of a pharmacist. My first attempt at fitting a truss was one of the most stressful things I have ever done. Even now my heart sinks at the very thought of the job. Nothing I had done at university prepared me for the sight that greeted me when I met my first scrotal hernia.

A hernia is basically a projection of part of an organ, usually the intestine or bowel, through the front muscular wall of the abdominal cavity. For one reason or another the muscle wall tears and a mass of tissue pokes out through the resulting hole. This swelling is often seen in the crease where the top of the leg meets the abdomen and that is called an inguinal hernia.

Both men and women can get hernias but they are more often seen with men. In forty years I have only ever dealt with one woman with a hernia. That was the case of a pregnant patient with a hernia right on her navel. This type of rupture is termed an umbilical hernia and is probably caused by the pressure of the foetus growing inside her and causing the muscle wall to tear.

This patient had to wear a truss with a large pad very carefully until her confinement. Then after her baby was born the pressure inside her abdomen was much less and I believe the tear was surgically repaired later.

A scrotal hernia on the other hand occurs when the lump of tissue, usually a bit of the bowel, protrudes down into the scrotal sac. The resultant swelling looks horrible and would, I imagine, be most uncomfortable.

Hernias are uncomfortable at best and can be life-threatening if they become strangulated. A strangulated hernia is one that can't be reduced, that is pushed back through the hole in the muscle. This leads to damage to the protruding tissue, damage to its blood supply and possibly to death. My very first hernia patient had a strangulated scrotal hernia.

The prescription, handed in by a woman on behalf of her husband, called simply for a truss. There was no further detail written on the form. I asked the lady to send her husband in to see me as he would have to be measured for the truss.

In the meantime I would have to contact the doctor for more details. What sort of truss for a start? There are two main types. What sort of hernia had the doctor diagnosed? The position, right or left or double I could see for myself when the patient arrived.

'He won't like coming in,' the patient's wife said. 'I had enough trouble getting him to go to the doctor in the first place.

Can't you just give me what you think he needs? You're supposed to be the experts!'

I looked at her sadly and shook my head.

'Look,' I said. 'I'll show you what the truss looks like and you will see why I can't guess what he needs. Come round to the fitting room.'

In the fitting room I laid out six trusses in a row on the couch. I put down a right, a left and a double of each of the two basic types. A spring truss consists of a strong metal bar inside a padded tube curved to fit over the hips and be strapped down between the legs. Pads of varying shapes are attached where needed. This type of truss is not used very often in my experience.

The elastic band truss is the type more often used. It looks quite frankly like a length of army surplus webbing with one or two pads screwed onto it in appropriate postions. An extra piece of webbing, often called a rat's tail because that's what it looks like, is also sewn onto the pad or pads. This strap secures the belt by going down between the legs and is then fixed to a loop on the belt behind the patient's back.

The important thing is to keep the pad firmly in place on top of the hernia and this three-way tension of the rat tail and the belt itself fitted over the hips should hold it securely. The pad must not slip or the bulge of tissue will escape out of the hole in the muscle and get pinched by the pad as the patient moves around. This will be very painful and could cause even more internal damage.

'So you can see that I need to know which type of belt your husband requires,' I said to the suddenly quiet woman. 'And also which size. There are a lot of different sizes. It isn't just a waist measurement, we have to get it right. We do keep a few commonly used sizes in stock here but if he's of a particularly big or small build we may have to order a suitable one. Then there are the different shaped pads as well depending on what he needs.'

The patient's wife had gone a bit pale at the sight of all these strange objects and she sat on the couch for a while. I fetched her a glass of water to drink then she left.

A couple of hours later her husband arrived. He looked annoyed and again demanded to know why he had to come and fetch this thing.

'You could have given it to my wife,' he moaned. 'I've got plenty of work to do you know!'

As this was my first attempt at fitting a truss Archie came into the fitting room with me and the patient. It wasn't a very big room and soon we were linked together as if in a rugby scrum. The patient, still reluctant to co-operate, finally removed his trousers and pants and lay down on his back on the couch.

In the meantime, we had discovered from the surgery that the doctor hadn't actually diagnosed what type of hernia was present. Personally I don't think he even examined the man properly but just scribbled a prescription for a truss and left it to us to sort out. I was to learn that this attitude was not uncommon. Doctors don't seem to like dealing with hernias either. Archie and I examined the patient and soon decided this was a scrotal hernia.

The most important thing before fitting the truss is to ensure that the hernia can be reduced. That is, the swelling can be put back through the tear in the muscle. You have to do that before fitting the truss or else the pad will pinch the protruding organ and cause further damage.

The only way to reduce a hernia is to manipulate the swelling between your fingers, gently trying to push the tissue back into place. Imagine trying to ease a small plastic bag filled with firm-ish jelly through a small slit which clamps itself shut every time you put any pressure on it.

Well, Archie tried and the patient yelped a couple of times. Then we showed him how and he tried to do it himself, and then I tried. We had a rest then we all tried again. The hernia would not be reduced.

All three of us were getting hot, sweaty and nowhere. Archie went to phone the doctor to break the news to him that his patient would have to be referred back. Meanwhile I explained that we would not be able to fit the truss if we couldn't reduce the hernia.

The patient was annoyed, getting angry and frustrated, until I described the painful death he might suffer if we did go ahead in the circumstances. He went very quiet until Archie returned. It had been decided that we should refer the patient back to his doctor.

A few days later another prescription for a truss arrived in the dispensary. It was made out to a new patient we didn't know. I picked up the form from the pile waiting to be dispensed and went out of the dispensary to look for the patient.

'Mr Gwatkin?' I asked and a man standing right by the counter nodded. Good I thought, the patient himself all present and correct. Hoping for a simple job this time, I led him round to the fitting room.

'Come in please Mr Gwatkin,' I said. 'We just need to find out which size is needed.'

The man nodded and followed me into the fitting room. I showed him what a truss looked like and explained that they came in a variety of sizes. He didn't say a word as I asked him to remove his trousers and underpants and lie down flat on his back on the couch.

When he was in position I started to take the measurement I needed to work out the size of his truss. I had just worked the tape measure around his back, over the crest of his hips and was aiming for the pubic bone when he spoke.

'I don't know if my brother will be the same size as me,' he said. I stared speechlessly, the world seemed to stop. 'Would it be better if he came to see you and got measured himself?' I swallowed hard and nodded.

'Yes please,' was all could manage.

That was another lesson learned. As a pharmacist this time as much as a manager. Make sure the person you're dealing with is the person you think they are!

We heard some days later that the earlier patient with the strangulated scrotal hernia had been admitted to hospital for an emergency operation to repair his hernia. Fortunately everything went well and he was home and soon back to work without further problems. To be fair he did come back in and thank us in the most friendly fashion with a bottle of whisky. Needless to say that disappeared without trace into Archie's office.

*

Occasionally I had to measure people for elastic stockings. This is nowhere near as hair-raising as truss fitting and has its own moments of fun. Usually Mrs Moore or Janet did the job and they were very good at it. It was another thing you never learn at university so they showed me how to take the necessary measurements and kindly, I suppose, let me practice on their patients.

Measuring someone for elastic stockings should be a fairly straightforward job as long as the patient rests with their feet up for a while to reduce the swelling in their veins before you take the measurement.

There always seems to be a great deal of confusion with what the patient expects versus what the NHS provides in the way of support stockings. The styles and colours didn't change for years and neither did the materials. What your grandmother found acceptable to wear in the post-war years certainly wouldn't suit the modern woman. Patients couldn't see why they should have to wear such dowdy looking stockings.

It is only in recent years that a slightly wider choice of colours has appeared. You can even get black stockings on the NHS now! Tights were very much in fashion at that time in the 60's and our patients could not see why they weren't allowed to have tights on the National Health Service. The simple answer is that the NHS will not pay for them. Most people think everything they have on prescription is free but somewhere along the way it has to be paid for and the NHS will only pay for what it specifies.

Men also have to wear elastic stockings sometimes but by far the majority of supplies were made to women. More properly called graduated compression hosiery, the stockings were supplied as lightweight, standard and heavy. Nowadays we call them, Class I, Class II and Class III. The higher the number, the stronger the support.

The term graduated refers to the fact that the support, that is the strength, in the material is greatest around the ankle and eases as you go up the leg. They are most often used for support when the patient suffers with varicose veins. Taking the necessary measurements results in properly fitting stockings but many patients assume that telling us a shoe size will do!

I still love to see the look on a woman's face when she is given a National Health suspender belt. The design of these vital pieces of equipment hasn't changed since the NHS was invented just after the end of the Second World War. In fact, I believe the design of these suspender belts was influenced, like the elastic truss, by the need to use up lots of army surplus webbing after the war. Dorothy Perkins or Ann Summers, they ain't. Sexy? Forget it! There is not a stitch of lace or a frill in sight. Having said that though, those beauties would be very useful if you ever feel the need to strap a pistol securely to your thigh.

*

There was a song recorded, I think, by the late John Denver called "Some days are diamonds, some days are stone". That neatly summed up those first few weeks in my new job. The first truss fitting was definitely in the stone category as was that old chap's corn plaster but just a few days later a diamond turned up in the pharmacy.

Betty had retired and Archie returned to the sales floor to spent more time in the dispensary. He should have been within sight and hearing of the dispensary anyway, by law, but seemed happy to leave more and more work to me.

A new girl, Mary, was employed to replace Betty and began her training. She was very nervous to start with especially after she had served that customer who asked for C-film and for a while tended to refer almost every customer's question to one of the rest of us to be on the safe side.

During one blazing hot day in early September an attractive young woman came in to ask for something to put on a rash. I happened to be standing nearby and Mary passed her on to me.

'A rash you said?'

'Yes,' the young woman replied. 'It is getting very itchy and red. I've only just noticed it today but it does feel sore. I haven't put anything on it yet. I wanted to ask you what was the best thing to use first.'

'Very wise,' I commented and asked. 'Where is the rash?

The young lady was wearing a pair of very brief shorts and a pretty white blouse. Just right for such a hot day. The blouse was buttoned up to leave a V-shaped opening at the neck. It was buttoned up to about level with the centre of her bra. At least, where the centre of the bra would have been if she had worn one. This was swinging sixties remember.

'Just here,' she said and to my surprise began to unbutton the blouse. Starting at the bottom button she continued slowly upwards. Later, Janet was to claim that my eyes stood out like chapel hat pegs but I sincerely believe I remained composed and professional at all times. I looked around expecting to see someone with a camera. Surely this was a setup, possibly a test by those very girls I'd been warned about on my first day.

At last the girl stopped, leaving the top button still done up. She looked into my eyes and smiled prettily. She knew what an effect she was having. Then she turned sideways to show me the rash along the top of her shorts. It was, of course, a simple sweat rash and I sold her a suitable soothing cream but my word she made my day, bless her.

5

As well as getting to know the staff and our regular customers I also met the occasional visitor to the Barnsgrove pharmacy. There were four of them that I particularly remember, each for a different reason.

The first of this small group of new acquaintances was known to everyone else simply as Ash. He was a semi-retired pharmacist who very occasionally did a day as a relief manager. He did as little actual work as possible mind you and I was to discover that wasn't his only bad habit. Ash was a heavy smoker, the girls told me, and I assumed that was where his nickname came from. In that I was only partly right.

Archie had to take a day off for some reason or other and announced to general dismay that Ash would be covering for him.

'Ugh! he's disgusting,' was all Janet would say adding with a grimace, 'You'll see,' when I asked about him.

Ash was truly a heavy smoker, a chain smoker of the really heavy tar cigarettes. He and his clothes stank of smoke. Even back in the 1960s we knew smoking killed you. I had seen enough pictures of diseased lungs while at university to put me off smoking and I just couldn't understand why an apparently intelligent man, after all he was a pharmacist, would carry on puffing away as he did.

Whenever possible during the day Ash slipped out of the dispensary and into the yard behind the shop to light up his cigarette. He was rarely able to finish his smoke before someone wanted him to check something, come to the phone or give the benefit of his knowledge to a customer in the shop.

With every interruption he sighed and came back into the dispensary. On the way in he would invariably remember he still had a cigarette in his hand and put it down somewhere safe. He obviously thought he would go back to finish it after dealing with whatever we wanted him for.

Sometimes he was right inside the dispensary before he remembered that he had a cigarette in his mouth. Once in a while one of us had to give him a nudge to remind him or he'd have gone out into the shop with it.

The smell of his cigarette followed him everywhere anyway so it was obvious to any customer what he'd been doing. The rest of us were certainly not allowed to smoke in the dispensary. Even Ash knew he should draw the line at appearing in front of the customers with a cigarette in his hand.

His technique when leaving the cigarette temporarily was to stand the thing up on end so that it continued to smoulder away while waiting for him to return. As it burned it deposited a small cone of ash on the shelf.

Frequently he forgot the cigarette he'd left standing and lit another one out in the yard after dealing with the query. The forgotten fag would slowly turn into a pile of ash to be found later by one of the dispensers.

Those scattered cones of ash were the reason for his nickname. No wonder the staff thought him disgusting, not to mention a danger to everyone else. Secondary smoking or breathing other people's smoke wasn't known to be bad in those days but Ash was highly rated as a fire risk.

*

Many of our standard mixtures for dispensing came in bulk packs in those far-off days. Sometimes we had to make our own but many of them were delivered ready-made in large brown bottles holding two litres of liquid medicine. These bottles were known as winchesters after the old Anglo-Saxon scale of measurements defined in the days of King Edgar during the tenth century. In his time the capital of England was the city of Winchester and that is where the standard measures of volume such as the bushel, peck and gallon were held.

By stocking these regularly used mixtures in bulk, we didn't have to make up small quantities for each individual prescription. As we often dispensed the same thing several times a day, this saved time for us and meant the patient didn't have to wait while the medicine for his or her prescription was made up from scratch.

A representative from one of the well-known drug companies came in one morning to tell us about some new product or other. He must have been too old to stir Amy's interest or indeed her hormones as she soon disappeared for her tea break.

Just before going out however Amy had opened a new winchester of Kaolin and Morphine Mixture and had poured 200ml into a bottle ready for a prescription. She had placed the winchester on the dispensary bench and, having attached a label to the bottle to complete the prescription, left it on the workbench to be checked.

Before starting on his spiel about the latest wonder product from his company the rep mentioned that he had been suffering with an upset stomach on and off for a few days.

'Would you mind if I borrow a dose of Kaolin and Morphine?' he asked, spotting the winchester that Amy had left on the bench.

Now I have never understood the concept of borrowing a dose of medicine. Would he be returning it in some form or another later? Would I want to see it coming back in any such a form? Anyway, many people seem to think they can borrow medicines from the dispensary and he was no exception.

Without waiting for an answer he picked up the winchester. Kaolin itself is a powder with a rather chalky appearance and is suspended in the liquid part of the mixture. It doesn't actually dissolve but settles down to a deposit in the bottom of the bottle until shaken. That is why you have to shake it well before you measure out your dose. Otherwise you would get the wrong proportion of kaolin to 'morphine'.

The rep knew this and gave the winchester a really good shake. It was a hearty shake. A good hefty shake. He really put his back into it. That was when we discovered that Amy hadn't tightened the top back onto the winchester. A fair proportion of almost two litres of the Kaolin and Morphine took to the air.

Displaying a rarely seen but decent moment of agility, I stepped from under the arching fluid. Sadly our visitor received most of it on top of his head, on his face, his shoulders, his suit and his shoes. The rest went over the shelves, the workbench and the floor.

Kaolin and Morphine mixture is dreadful stuff. It smells unpleasant, it dries to a horrible powdery mess and it is virtually impossible to get out of your clothes if you spill it. No matter how much you wash there will always be a chalky residue. We were still picking lumps of the stuff off the shelves in the dispensary weeks later. The floor never again looked quite as clean as one would like it to do but at least it got rid of the rep.

He wiped off as much as he could, spent an hour or so in the staff toilet trying to clean himself up and presumably several more hours later at home attempting to rid his car seat of the stuff. I bet his car still stinks even now. That'll teach them to think they can borrow stock from the dispensary!

*

Archie was blessed with an excellent staff. They had been handpicked, as he often said. Indeed, over the years he had taken on two or three generations from some of the families in town.

I remember him saying how he knew that he'd been in the branch for a long time when a young girl came in for a Saturday job. She looked familiar and he asked if he knew her from somewhere else. She told him that he had taken on her mother as a Saturday girl when she herself was at school and that her grandmother had also worked for him when he first came to the town. Archie felt, he said, so terribly old that day.

He knew his staff well and appreciated their efforts. The business ran smoothly and we had few complaints either from our customers or head office. I had thought him a bit messy and disorganised when I first arrived. He never bothered to tidy his office in all the time I knew him but I soon realised that he knew his job and, having trained his staff well, let them get on with their work with the minimum of fuss. Having said that he had little patience with those who wasted his time or interfered with the smooth running of his systems.

Like most companies we were blessed with a head office. One often wonders what they do there and one certainly wonders who takes on some of the aspiring middle managers I've met over the years. Such was the lack of effect from our head office and its ways that I had worked at the branch for about three months before someone mentioned that we had something called a Territorial General Manager. This was shortened to TGM.

Incidentally, I've noticed more than once over the years that big companies love to shorten titles and invent acronyms. Often, I reckon, they invent new systems or projects specially to fit a new acronym which was thought up by someone in head office with nothing better to do.

You can picture a group of such people meeting on a cold, wet, miserable Wednesday afternoon in February. They will be desperate for someone to say something to pass the time and perhaps that someone will mention that he's thought of an exciting word. Perhaps they've had an inter-departmental Scrabble competition and wonder what to do with the letter tiles left at the end. It might even be a significant word as far as the company is concerned such as the name of a founder or the home town of one of the directors.

The one who thought up the word will be overcome with excitement and everyone else will try to make up the name of a new project to fit the letters. If the department head's christian name was Fred for example several hours of meetings might be necessary before someone comes up with the big new idea.

'Fred stands for Fast Reliable Efficient Dispensing,' he or she will say proudly and all the others present will congratulate themselves. Pay rises for the committee will be approved and bonuses paid. The new motto will be printed on signs and letters to be sent out to all the branches. Gullible staff will pin such things up on staff notice boards and quote 'Fred' to each other whenever possible.

Archie would have filed such things straight into the waste bin and quite rightly too. He knew his staff provided a fast reliable and efficient service and didn't need anyone else to tell him. They knew they were doing a good job because he told them so, and thanked them.

We were approaching Christmas by now and it seemed the TGM, or the 'Chosen One', as Archie called him, would be expected to grant us a visit. I suppose the idea was for him to wish us a merry Christmas and thank us for coping so well with all the extra work that the season brings. Mrs Moore called this paragon 'The Boy' and it soon became obvious why she did so when he turned up.

I was in the dispensary when 'The Boy' arrived, except of course I didn't know who he was. A smartly dressed young lad carrying a briefcase walked straight into the dispensary without a word. For obvious security reasons we didn't allow anybody to wander into the dispensary uninvited. Even in those far-off days of innocence before we'd heard of terrorists or suicide bombers there were occasional attempts at robbery or violence..

'And where do you think you're going?' I asked while stepping in front of him to block his progress.

Mrs Moore turned to see who I was speaking to. I'm sure I caught a new look of respect for me in her eyes as she introduced the man. I say man but he looked even younger than me. He was one of those people who manage to look just so clean and shiny. No drop of sweat would ever dare to appear on his brow, his handshake was limp and soft and his smile utterly false.

Wandering into the dispensary, he stood in the very place where he would be most in the way and proceeded to speak to us as if he were the most important deity in our miserable lives. And he had ignored my intervention completely.

His suit was immaculate, his tie perfectly tied and, as Mrs Moore commented later, he looked like his mum polished him before sending him out to work each day. Even his briefcase, which was beautiful, was carried like a badge of office. A royal handbag could not have carried such an aura of majesty. He was very young to be a TGM and, in Mrs Moore's opinion, he had been promoted far beyond his abilities.

Archie arrived in the dispensary and it soon became clear that 'The Boy' had no interest in the staff or what we did. The idea that he should be thanking us for our hard work had never entered his mind. His whole existence revolved around pie-charts, graphs, budgets and targets. I remember thinking that if ever anyone needs a good slap, this is him.

Archie had a well run branch. Everything was going to budget and all the targets were, well, on target. Yet this youth couldn't be bothered to thank us or even take an interest in what we were doing. Archie's face became pink then red in his exasperation as this idiot blethered on. I thought a fuse was going to blow but 'The Boy' suddenly turned to Mrs Moore.

'Margaret,' he said. No-one else ever dared to call her Margaret. Until that moment I didn't even know her first name was Margaret. 'You have been here a very long time. You must have seen a great many changes.'

'Yes,' she said warily.

'And there are many changes to come,' he trilled on without pause. 'We, the company, intend to push the boundaries of the business. There will be new lines, special promotions, a plethora of new ideas. The company will reach out to our customers and our staff, we will all grow together as we go into the future. Ah, the future.' His eyes closed blissfully. We looked at one another and wondered how much more of this nonsense we could stomach.

'Now Margaret.' he continued without even looking at her. None of us dared to look at her either. 'The future. Where do you see us in say two years time? Where will you be in all this?'

There was a short pause as if Mrs Moore was considering whether to hit him with the tablet counter gripped in her hand.

'I shall be over the fields walking my dog,' she said quietly but firmly. The world seemed to stop and we all held our breath. He stared at her as if he'd noticed her for the first time, as if he was arriving with a jolt from his other world. 'I will be retired in less than two years time as you should know,' she explained in a calm, even but firm voice. 'I shan't give a thought to what you or the company is doing after that.'

Janet told me later that 'The Boy' had, during a previous 'royal' visit, confirmed that Mrs Moore must retire at her 60th birthday in line with the company policy at the time. She had made it clear that she would have been happy to continue to work beyond that date if only part time. You would think the company would appreciate having the further use of her knowledge and experience but big companies don't seem to think like that.

Up in the office a few days later, Archie showed me a memo he'd received which said in effect that the TGM thought they could save money by employing a new, younger dispenser after Mrs Moore had gone.

'That's the sort of thing we're up against these days,' he said grimly. 'You'll find more and more of it in the future as well. Those clods in head office seem to think that all the dispensing could be done by well-trained chimpanzees. Then I bet they'd try to cut their banana ration!'

No wonder Mrs Moore didn't give a thought to what happened after her retirement. She had done her best, had helped to train a new generation of dispensers and supported her colleagues. And, I would suggest, how typical of the attitude of those who tried to impose their daft ideas instead of leading us.

*

Until I completed my post-graduate work and registered with the Pharmaceutical Society I could not be left in charge of a pharmacy. This meant that if Archie was absent for some reason, a holiday say, a day off or illness then a relief manager or locum pharmacist would arrive. There were several of these working in the area but we usually had the same chap each time.

'Hi Paul. I'm Doug,' he said the first time we met and almost pulled my hand off my wrist with his handshake. 'How's it going?'

Doug was a young, recently qualified pharmacist. In fact he had spent his post-graduate year in that very branch of the company only two years before me. I remember being very impressed with his calm nature. The day just simply eased along in his presence, nothing flustered him and not even the most awkward or abusive customer could rush him. He knew what he was doing and got on with it, quietly and efficiently. The majority of our customers liked him. We all liked the man and looked forward to the days he spent with us. Even Mrs Moore took to him and treated him, in spite of his youth, as an equal.

However, Doug did have one habit which occasionally caused a gasp of surprise, a quiet snigger at the back of the dispensary and a look of despair from Mrs Moore.

When a prescription had been dispensed to his satisfaction, Doug would put the items in a bag, seal it with exactly half an inch of sellotape and stride out to the counter. One day he explained to me that by using half an inch of sellotape rather than a staple to seal the bag he was actually saving the company a great deal of money. I still have no idea whether he was serious about that.

He always assumed the patient or their representative would be waiting for their medication but we always had to check that we were giving the correct medicine to the right person. This is, incidentally, often a problem for us. People seem to think that their prescription is the only medicine we deal with and assume that we know all their names. The usual method, and the safest, is to call out the patient's name to identify them and then check their address before handing over the medicine.

Doug's method was very simple and, as with everything he did, very efficient. He always called out the title and surname then followed that up with the first name and surname as a reminder. Thus, for example, he would call out 'Mrs Smith. Mrs Joan Smith'. There could, as he so rightly said, be a whole bunch of different Mrs Smiths waiting for their medication. You must find the right one. The address check would find the right Mrs Joan Smith if there should happen to be more than one of those.

Usually the patient or whoever was collecting her medicine would answer or come forward and then Doug would confirm the address with them before handing over the bag with any suitable information they might need. He used this same system for everyone irrespective of age, title or sex.

Sometimes, however, there was an odd combination of titles or names. A mention of Miss Chance always raised a smile and whenever the Reverend Green's name was called someone invariably murmured 'In the library with the dagger' in reference to the game, Cluedo. However my favourite moment of all came when Doug called out the name of a small boy named Philip David Bates.

The pharmacy was even busier than normal that evening as there had been an outbreak of colds and flu in the area. A crowd of people were waiting for their medicines.

Several of them were chatting to their neighbours in the queue so, raising his voice above the hubbub, Doug called out 'Master Bates...' He paused amid a stunned silence broken only by Janet's giggle.

6

The pace of work in the pharmacy increased drastically as we entered the month of December. Christmas on the High Street always means a lot of hard work for all the staff. More stock to move, more customers to serve and more paperwork to account for it all. We had taken on a couple of temporary girls but, as usual, it was the rest of us who carried the burden.

I hadn't realised before starting work that all the ordering of stock for Christmas is done at the height of summer. In future years I was to spend many a hot sweaty afternoon in June working out sales targets and ordering budgets and then trying to get my over-eager staff to stick to then. Faced with catalogues full of the stock available everyone seems to think it was Christmas (yes I know it is!) and orders whatever they like unless you watch them carefully. It is very easy to exceed your budget.

Even so, when the stock arrives at the store during October and November every nook and corner in the building becomes stuffed with boxes and bags. The whole sales floor has to be reorganised to build Christmas displays. Everyone tends to get pressured, over-excited, sometimes argumentative. Especially if one person thinks another is taking over their share of the shelf space or not pulling their weight. The pressure really starts to build as the Christmas rush gets under way.

On top of all that, December is always one of the busiest times of the year for dispensing. Every year Christmas brings an outbreak of some illness or other along with the usual coughs and colds and all the time the regular patients still need their repeat medication. The queues build up and the piles of prescriptions to be dispensed get higher. It is a most stressful time of the year.

In spite of all the extra work, the struggle to keep the shelves filled, the surge of customers, the never-ending search for sufficient change and all the dreaded paperwork and sorting out afterwards, most of us enjoy working at this time of the year. For many of us however the highlight of working at this season is the staff Christmas party.

Over the last forty years I have experienced just about every type of Christmas do possible. I have spent a quiet evening in a Chinese restaurant with a group of staff that included a dispenser with toothache and a newly widowed cleaner, eaten an exotic range of pub meals and had various hotel dinners which came with and without dancing.

I recall a staff party that involved a pub quiz night where the competition became so fierce that we ended up with a series of bizarre 'Its-a-knockout' type games to decide a winner. How no-one broke a leg, or worse, is still a mystery to me.

One year we allowed a Saturday girl to book her brother's band for the after-dinner dancing. Four lads with absolutely no talent hammering the life out of three guitars and a set of drums left an impression such that the following year we went to the other extreme. A trio of seventy-year olds playing between them a piano accordion, a saxophone and one solitary snare drum entertained us with sundry war songs and 'music from the films'.

'Pity they weren't silent movies,' someone muttered in despair.

I wasn't sure what to expect this first Christmas but it turned out to be a rather posh do in a large hotel. An evening of dinner and dancing was promised. A proper band had been booked. Well, a quintet of sorts. It would be party frocks for the women and jackets and ties for the men, I was told.

'Apart from Archie, I'm the only man going,' I complained.

'Husbands and boyfriends, wives and girlfriends are all invited.' Amy fluttered her eyelashes and pouted. 'Who are you bringing then?'

'Archie's wife will be there,' Janet noticed my panic-stricken face and butted in. 'You know about our little Christmas tradition don't you?'

'What little tradition would that be?' I asked cautiously.

'The current year's student has to start the dancing with Archie's wife,' she replied with a sweet smile. 'You'll like that.'

'What's she like?' I asked. Archie's wife never came into the pharmacy. I has asked about her once before and had been told that she spent her time galloping around on horses, chasing foxes, shooting squirrels and scaring the life out of the other members of the Women's Institute. I hadn't thought that last one possible but then I didn't know whether to believe everything those girls told me.

'She's a big strong woman,' Amy smirked. 'You'll have your hands full there.' She wandered off into the shop.

'Is all this true?' I asked Janet. 'Or are you two just winding me up again.'

'Most of it is true,' she smiled. 'You'll only have to dance with Mrs Johns once though. Unless you want another go at it of course.'

'It sounds as though once will be enough.' I paused then cleared my throat. 'Are you coming with anyone special?'

'Actually, I'm not coming at all. I hadn't mentioned it to anybody yet,' she said with a sad little smile. 'My boyfriend, David, has his works do the same evening and he wants us to go to that. Sorry.'

A cold frosty evening greeted me as I left my flat to walk to the hotel for the Christmas party. The Royal Victoria Hotel had been built at the height of the Victorian Age when the town had set out to attract visitors to sample the curative properties of its spa waters. The local spa was promoted on the back of the popular water treatments available at Malvern which is about thirty miles away.

Two doctors, Dr James Wilson who gained his knowledge of the water cure in Germany and Dr James Manby Gulley who wrote a popular book on Neuropathy, opened their centre in Malvern in 1842. Many famous people soon gathered there and Malvern's spa and social scene was soon world famous.

One of the the water cures involved wrapping the patients in wet sheets and covering them in eiderdowns then, when unwrapped, they were given a cold shower and a rub down. The patients were then sent on a long hike up the hills and told to drink a glass of water at each of the wells which spring from various points on the hillside. The really infirm patients were sent up on the backs of donkeys.

The cold showers apparently came in two forms namely the normal descending douche where the victim (sorry patient) stood under a stream of cold water. The alternative was known as the ascending douche. This was a powerful upward pointing jet of cold water which I'd rather not think about. Patients were also put on a strict diet with no alcohol. It all sounds terrific fun.

Something similar was offered in our local spa for a few years in the mid-1800s but it was never as popular as the Malvern treatment. The Royal Victoria Hotel had gently faded over the ensuing years although it still had a certain grand air about it.

The mineral spring with its magical properties was now hidden under a manhole in the pavement on the opposite side of the road. A local artist had produced a neat roundel depicting two nymphs dancing around a fountain which had been incorporated into the paving slabs nearby. Otherwise it had faded from the town's memory.

Queen Victoria stayed at the hotel once, hence the name, and there, in the entrance of the hotel next to the reception desk, was a large glass case containing an old visitors book. The book was displayed open to show her Majesty's signature and her comment, 'Perfectly satisfied'. Hoping that I would be similarly satisfied with the coming meal, I watched as the happy staff with their husbands and boyfriends passed by.

Feeling a little lonely, I dithered in the doorway for a moment then followed the wonderful scent of cooking food into the dining room. The hotel had made an effort of sorts to decorate their ballroom although the tree decorations looked as though Queen Victoria would recognise them instantly.

Inside the dining room I bumped into Mrs Moore and her husband. I learned something else that night. Knowing someone by working with them day after day in the same environment often means that you only know one part of their personality. The working person, as it were. Mrs Moore was a good example of how people can have such different characters depending on when you meet them. At work she was serious, almost dour, and looked quite plain. You wouldn't look at her twice.

I almost didn't recognise her that evening. A glamorous long silvery dress, carefully applied makeup and strappy, high-heeled shoes, knocked years off her. The vision was completed by her hair, rich and glowing, piled high with many curls and waves. She certainly didn't look to be almost 59 years old and nearing retirement. I'm sure she read my mind and laughed at me as she introduced her husband.

Mr Moore was very smartly dressed, a prosperous looking businessman. I felt quite dowdy standing between them. He ran the local Austin car dealership and we chatted about the latest models. Mrs Moore mentioned my old A35 and he smiled sympathetically.

'Pop in and see me sometime,' he said. Ever the salesman, I thought. 'We'll see what we can do about something nicer for you. When they make you a branch manager you'll need a suitable vehicle.'

Archie stood by the bar with a veritable amazon of a woman by his side. This must be Mrs Archie, I reckoned. She was taller than me, well over six foot I'd say, and built like the proverbial barn door. They beckoned me over to join them. I was almost there before I noticed another younger woman dressed in a beautiful green gown hidden behind the bulk of Archie's wife. Archie introduced his guests.

'Come and meet my wife,' he said. 'Hermione, this is Paul. He's our post-grad student this year.'

'Hello, nice to meet you,' I said and winced as she crushed my hand.

'And this is our niece, Lucy,' he added fondly. 'She's been staying with us for a week or so. Then she's off home to Scotland on Sunday for Hogmanay. We're quite jealous.'

Lucy smiled and said hello. She had the most delicious Scots accent. It was soft and sweet, with a suggestion of heathery mountains and sun-sparkled lochs. Her long dark hair bounced along her bare freckled shoulders and her deep green eyes made me think of how much I'd love to have porridge for breakfast in the morning.

As the only two people without partners we were seated together when we settled down to eat. She was wonderful company and I did my best to entertain her. Later I got the chance to dance with her, but just the once.

I danced with Archie's wife as well, again only once. I had been taught a bit of ballroom dancing at school but didn't consider myself much of a dancer. Mrs Johns didn't understand that old fashioned concept of the man leading the woman but we spun round with as elegant a waltz as either of us could have managed in the circumstances.

My duty done, I returned to my seat and looked forward to spending the rest of the evening with Lucy. She was, I learned, training to be a teacher. We seemed to be getting on very well but unfortunately Amy chose that night of all nights to break up with her latest boyfriend.

I was aware of an argument going on in the bar after dinner. It started quietly at first, just muttering and murmuring in the distance as the others tried to calm the pair down. Then we could hear someone crying, then shouts and finally a red faced young man burst out through the door and slammed it shut behind him.

There was a moment of silence as everyone wondered what to do. I heard someone say that he'd waited until he'd had his dinner before he went and remembered that the cost of the evening had been shared by a small donation from the company but mostly by the staff themselves.

Amy ran across the room and threw herself onto my lap. Her arms went round my neck as she rammed her face into my neck and I felt her tears running down inside the collar of my shirt. Her body shook as she sobbed.

'Er... Steady on,' I wasn't sure what to do. Why pick on me? Surely she didn't imagine I had any feelings for her. Had she read more than I'd thought into that one kiss in the cellar? That was weeks ago! I had tried to distance myself from her ever since but she was notoriously flighty. What romantic nonsense had been fermenting away in her mind? What had been said between her and that departing boyfriend? Would he hold me responsible for their breaking up? Did he punch his weight?

Her sobbing increased and I realised that in trying to comfort her my hand was caressing her bare thigh where her already short dress had ridden up. Lucy's mouth dropped open and I felt her eyes burning into my hand. I removed it from the hot thigh and tried to push Amy upright but she clung on tightly.

The band started playing and with an audible sigh of relief everyone turned away from the awful spectacle to start dancing again. Lucy got up and moved away to sit by her aunt.

'Steady on,' I said to Amy again but with no more effect.

I didn't get chance to say anything else to Lucy and after a while, Archie and his wife took her home. The look that Archie's wife gave me as they went suggested that her opinion of students and the way they carry on with her husband's staff had been reinforced.

Fortunately for me, but too late for my evening with Lucy, a couple of the other girls came over and persuaded Amy to go to the ladies room with them and tidy herself up. I made my escape when they'd gone and hoped they would make sure she got home safely.

*

Everyone was a bit quiet at work in the morning. Fortunately it was a very busy day and no-one had time to comment or ask questions about the evening's events. Janet looked puzzled but I suppose someone filled her in with the story at some point. Amy sniffled and crept around in silence. Archie didn't say anything at all until just before we closed. We happened to be alone in the dispensary when he turned to me.

'A small piece of advice for you,' he said quietly. 'You'll find life much easier if you don't get too friendly with the staff. Always keep a distance between you and them. Not a wide gulf by any means but just enough of a space. Don't set up barriers between you of course. That would be wrong. Just let them know that you are the boss. Then they'll know their place and you will know yours. You can't be a manager in any other way. Manager or mate. You have to choose.'

I felt that he knew I wasn't like Gary and that I hadn't encouraged Amy in any way. He chose to deal with the problem in a most sensible way. Those were among the wisest words I ever heard him say. I am most grateful for his understanding.

7

Early in the new year I was sent on the first of a set of management training days organised by head office. I can only recall two things from that first day which probably tells us something about much of the management training of the time.

The speakers were heavily influenced by those evangelist-type company organisation experts in America. There were quite a few of them around. They all seemed to have made films of their performances which we had to watch and in these they brought us such concepts as 'Mission Statements', 'Corporate Ideals', 'Bottom Up' organisations and 'Top Down' models.

I never did understand how you could have both of the last two. I don't think the company ever understood that either. In any case, they never seemed to take any notice of those of us who slaved away at the bottom of the heap.

One of those two things I did remember from the course was the speaker who showed us a method that we could use to train anyone to do anything. He explained his theory by making a paper tray from a small square piece of paper by folding it with an Origami technique.

First he told us in one go how to make the tray. It was just a blur of paper and gabbled instructions. He told us to have a go. We all made a mess of the job as we tried to remember his instructions and copy his work.

Then he demonstrated the same process step by step. We all followed him successfully. The message being, I think, that something learned logically, step by step, will be something learned properly.

Some time later I showed one of my daughters how to make a folded paper tray in the same way and now, thirty years on, she still remembers how to do it. I suppose that proves his point. I have forgotten however. That is an age thing!

Another speaker that day talked about leadership. He reminded us of the famous story about Ernest Shackleton's expedition to Antarctica and his glorious but failed attempt to walk to the South Pole. This took place in 1908, even before Captain Robert Scott and Raold Amundsen raced to that awful place.

When Shackleton had to give up and turn back to his base, his team was exhausted, sick and short of food. At one point they were sheltering in a tent with a gale howling outside and the temperature at 70 degrees below zero. They were rationed to only one biscuit each for a meal.

Shackleton noticed that one of his men was in a worse condition than the rest and offered the man his own biscuit. This action was held up as a magnificent example of good leadership. A man who truly cared for his team.

When I returned to work, the staff in the dispensary asked me what I'd learned from the course. After demonstrating how to make the tray by folding a piece of paper, I showed them, to their obvious disbelief, how useful it would be to store paperclips and similar things. Then I told them the story illustrating Ernest Shackleton's example of good leadership. They seemed quite impressed with my account of the expedition.

'If we were in that awful situation, snowed in, starving, freezing cold, in deadly danger and we had one biscuit each,' I queried. 'Would one of you give me your last biscuit if I needed it?'

There was a silence for a moment. Janet, Amy and Mrs Moore looked at each other. An unspoken debate appeared to be taking place. Thinking that they hadn't understood me, I was about to clarify my question when they appeared to come to a decision.

'What sort of biscuit would it be?' Janet suddenly asked before I spoke.

There was a further brief but thorough discussion before they announced their decision. Whether I was to be given that last biscuit depended on one thing and one specific thing only. What sort of biscuit would they have to give up? I was soon to know that I rated higher in their estimation than a fig roll or a Garibaldi biscuit but much lower than something like a milk chocolate digestive.

'I don't like fig rolls anyway,' added Amy with a shake of her head. 'Yuk!'

Several weeks later the girls were still offering me fig rolls and Garibaldi biscuits at tea time. I had already found my place in the world of pharmacy.

*

A letter arrived through the internal postal system in early May to inform me that I was to visit head office for two days. It was important, the writer said, that I should understand how the company was organised and the way that a head office supports its branches. Archie said he'd like to know as well.

We would also get to see something of the company's distribution system during a visit to one of the warehouses and be given an insight into the ways that new products were developed. The letter also informed me that I would be staying in a hotel overnight and that a small amount of money would be allowed to cover my travelling expenses.

Archie never did have much time for the company's head office or those who worked there. I discovered soon after my arrival at the branch that most of the paperwork in the "Maybe" tray originated in head office. He only troubled himself with what he considered necessary for the efficient running of his branch.

You must prioritise your workload, is the expression we would use in later years but Archie was well ahead of his time in many ways. He prioritised much of his paperwork straight into the waste paper bin.

'I can't imagine why it would take them two whole days to show you what they do in head office,' Archie muttered as he read my letter. He grunted again. 'I see they're putting you up at the New Bridgeford Hotel though. That's alright. I stayed there once when I had to go up for some reason or other. It isn't as new as it sounds but its not bad.'

*

'Is that you Paul?' The phone call arrived just as I came back into the dispensary after lunch. 'Pete Evans here.' Pete was another post-graduate student working at the company's branch in Marden Green, about twenty-five miles away. 'Have you been summoned to head office?'

'Yes I have, a week next Monday. I've had a letter this morning'

'Same here,' he replied. 'How are you travelling up?'

'I hadn't really thought about that yet, They've offered me a few quid for travelling expenses but I doubt it'll cover the fuel for my van or the train fare. That's typical!'

'I've been thinking,' Pete went on. 'If we went together in my car we could pool the expenses and cover the fuel. What do you think? I could pick you up outside the shop early enough to get us there for 9 o'clock.' I agreed. 'Pick you up at six then.' He hung up without further discussion. He was always in a hurry, our Pete.

*

The tour of head office that we had on the first day was as tedious as we'd expected. Then, back at the hotel, Pete and I found out that we'd be sharing a room. I had no problem with that until his alarm clock went off.

I rolled over in my bed and struggled to open my eyes. It was still dark but in the faint glow of street lights outside I could just about make out that Pete was getting dressed.

'It's still very dark,' I yawned. 'What time is it?'

'Oh sorry,' he said, bright as a button. 'I hoped to get away without waking you. Its about half past three.' I sat up straight and glared at the vague shape across the room.

'Half past three! What are you doing? They don't serve breakfast until seven thirty at the earliest.'

'A friend of mine, I knew him at school, lives a few miles from here. I spoke to him a couple of nights ago. He's organised a dawn chorus party and invited me. Do you want to come?'

'A dawn chorus party?' I repeated slowly and wondered if I was dreaming, or having a nightmare. 'Are you mad? We've got another boring day looking round the rest of head office today. I need my sleep.' I rolled over as he went on dressing and tried to concentrate on getting back to sleep.

'He lives on a farm,' Pete chatted away. For some reason he felt the need to tell me about his friend. 'Lovely place, his family owns it. Their ownership goes back generations, hundreds of years I'd bet. The idea is for a group of his friends to meet at four o'clock, before it gets light, and listen to the birds as they join in the dawn chorus. I did it last year. It is amazing.' I grunted and stayed where I was.

'And afterwards they all gather in the farmhouse kitchen for the most fantastic cooked breakfast you've ever seen, Their own bacon and sausages, free range eggs, homemade bread and butter, marmalade, everything and lots of it. Come on, you'll thank me later.'

'Oh alright,' I groaned. I was wide awake by now and he had started me thinking about that breakfast. 'I might as well come with you.'

We crept away from the hotel and drove out to the farm. There were, as far as I could make out, about twenty people in the darkness of the farmyard and we settled down on a variety of chairs and benches to await the performance.

I have to admit that I began to enjoy myself. I hadn't had much to do with bird watchers before that morning but, while I still don't prowl around in reed beds very often, this was to be the start of a lifelong interest in natural history.

The night was still dark, an orange-tinted three-quarter sized moon had just set behind the distant hills and a few stars twinkled overhead. I could just about make out the shape of a row of poplar trees across the field. It was quiet and dry but cold, very cold. I hadn't realised that early mornings could be so cold.

I leaned back in my deck chair and gazed up at the stars. A murmur of quiet conversation, the smell of mint humbugs and some chattering teeth were the only signs that I was not alone in the universe.

A sudden sharp call, an unexpectedly exotic beginning, came from a peacock in a neighbour's garden. Then a blackbird's alarm call which certainly woke up some robins. Within minutes three of them were singing. We had a robin to the left, a robin to the right and another in front. The blackbird joined in with what Pete's friend, Alan, called that nonchalant-leaning-against-the-chimney-easy-listening-sort-of-full-throated-warble, and we were off. Fortunately for me Alan gave us a whispered running commentary to identify the singers.

From the undergrowth a wren hurled a long rapid song. A mistle thrush, followed quickly by a song thrush meant we could compare their songs and the similar one of the blackbird. Each sounded clearly different now of course and lovely.

We sat listening to the countryside waking up around us for about an hour and a half. When a blackcap started singing Alan reminded us that they are known as the 'nightingale of the north' for their lovely song which can be heard all the way up to the Arctic tundra.

It felt a bit like the tundra had invaded that farmyard as a cold breeze swirled around the farmhouse so, as the sun lifted itself over the poplar trees, we set off for a walk to warm up and sharpen our appetites for breakfast.

Walking into a wood we found masses of bluebells and some gorgeous early purple orchids. We heard even more birdsong as well, such a mixture of sounds from a tiny goldcrest among some conifers to two buzzards soaring overhead.

A woodpecker was drumming in the distance. All three native woodpeckers; green, great spotted and lesser spotted woodpeckers make this noise and apparently the expert, like Alan and I suspect most of his friends, can tell which one it is from the length of time it drums. I would need a lot more practice.

We had to pass the time of day with some cows returning from milking before they let us through to the farmhouse for breakfast. This was taken around a huge wooden farmhouse table with plenty of tea, coffee and chat.

Then afterwards as it was still only eight o'clock we had an easy ride back to the hotel, a quick shower and change. I cannot for the life of me remember a better start to a day nor anything about the rest of the day at head office.

*

A few weeks later I attended yet another training course. This one lasted a whole week and involved the usual shambles of role playing. Why do they bother? When I arrived back at work I found a very different atmosphere in the dispensary.

A sombre mood, everyone crept around concentrating on their work, hardly daring to look at one another. Janet's face was very pale, almost white, her lips looked colourless and thin too. When I did catch her eye she looked away again quickly. She was quite clearly near to tears. This was very unlike her normal self. What was wrong? No-one said a word all morning.

Amy also looked downright ill. Her usual vacant far-away expression was reinforced by her slow, dreamlike movements. She made a couple errors with the first two prescriptions she was dealing with and seemed surprised when I pointed them out to her. As if she was looking at them for the first time. Archie looked strained and upset about something and Mrs Moore didn't seem to want to be there at all.

As I watched them carefully moving around each other silently and avoiding contact, I assumed that something major had gone wrong while I'd been away. Had we made a dispensing error? Had someone died? Was one of us in serious trouble? Was it me? I racked my brain in an attempt to remember anything that I might have done to cause such a terrible atmosphere.

When Amy went for her tea break and Archie had to go up to the office for some reason I took my chance and tackled Janet and Mrs Moore.

'What is the matter?' I asked quietly. 'Has something dreadful happened?'

'I'm leaving,' Janet said, tears ran down her face. 'Sorry.' She reached for a tissue and blew her nose.

'Leaving? Why?'

'I've been transferred to another branch.' she turned away. 'I'll tell you about it later.'

I looked across to Mrs Moore. She shook her head and make a face which I took to mean 'shut up!' so I carried on checking some prescriptions. We worked on in silence. Just before lunch time Janet nudged my arm.

'It looks like a nice day out there,' she nodded toward the shop front. 'Do you fancy putting your coat on and coming for a walk in the park when we go to lunch?'

'Sure.'

A chilly wind swirled around us in the park so we kept walking. The best of the summer flowers were coming up, filling out the patterns laid out in the formal beds. Normally I would have enjoyed a walk like that but we walked in silence. On our second time round the lily pond Janet took a deep breath and started her explanation.

'It was horrible,' she said. 'Archie had a letter from that twerp of a TGM. You remember him? He told Archie that the dispenser from the Greenlands branch had handed in her notice. She's getting married and moving away, I think. They haven't got another dispenser, not even a trainee. Their manager doesn't seem to have bothered to plan for a replacement and now they're in a mess.

'As the TGM pointed out, we have three dispensers here plus you until August. He also pointed out that we are the nearest branch to Greenlands and told Archie to choose one of us dispensers to transfer there, permanently, starting next Monday.'

'That is horrible,' I said and considered for a minute. 'Well, if it were up to me I'd send Amy. The boss must have realised that when Mrs Moore retires at the end of next year he'll need a reliable replacement. That would be you surely.'

'Thanks,' a faint smile at last. 'Maybe he would have decided that, if he'd had chance to stop and work it out. I don't know quite how it happened but the Amy and I ended up drawing straws. I lost.'

'You'll have to travel back and forth every day.' I said. 'That'll take you half an hour each time, at least.' She nodded silently.

'I suppose I'll just have to go. I'll try it for a bit but if I don't like it there I'll be leaving.' Her determined look showed that she meant it.

The next couple of days were horrible. We were all resigned to her leaving. Then around mid-morning on Thursday, the telephone rang and Archie picked up the receiver. He listened for a moment then snapped a short reply and put the receiver down with far more force than usual.

'Those blasted people in Greenlands want Janet over there as soon as possible,' he growled and looked at her. 'I don't suppose you've got your own transport?' Janet shook her head. 'We'll have to look up the bus times.'

Just then, one of the company van drivers arrived with a delivery of stock. Archie grabbed his arm.

'Are you going on to the Greenlands branch next?' he demanded.

'Yes,' the driver replied.

'Can you take one of my dispensers with you?' he asked. 'She has to get there as soon as she can. They're short of staff.' The man looked a bit surprised but nodded.

Thus it was that Janet was transferred just like a bit of company stock from one branch to another. Our parting was very quick. We crowded around the poor girl shaking her hand, giving her a hug, wishing her well. While she fetched her coat and handbag I dashed up to the tea room and hurried back with a small gift.

Her eyes were filling with tears and so were ours. It was a dreadful moment, an awful goodbye. A peck on the cheek and an instruction to 'keep in touch' and she was gone. I just managed to slip the gift into her bag as she went.

'Look at it later,' I said.

Janet left the company altogether a few months later. The travelling was too much, too awkward. She disliked her new manager and found another job. Archie was incandescent with rage.

'It takes a long time and a lot of money to train a dispenser,' he ranted. 'What a waste!'

I was thinking more in terms of how the rest of us had lost a good friend. I have never met a better dispenser, a more willing and able worker. It was such a shame to lose her and, to me, a prime example of how a company should never treat its staff. What would Ernest Shackleton have said? Another lesson in management as Janet would have said with one of her smiles.

Although we had only met for the first time the previous August and worked together for less than a year, I felt I had known Janet for ever. We had many a good chat during which we sorted out the world's problems and helped each other through the hectic day.

I had always known that I would be moving on after my year at Barnsgrove but I'd had fond thoughts of maybe going back there occasionally as a relief manager, like Doug. Or perhaps even one day I might return as the branch manager. Janet and I would work together again. It was not to be.

Much later, when I did become the manager of my own branch, one of my duties was to assess my staff. Each year I had to discuss with them their successes and failures. Then we had to set ourselves targets for the next year.

Along the way I evolved a private method of scoring their ability. I called it my 'Janet Scale'. With this I rated each member of staff's performance between one and ten with one being weak and ten equalling perfection.

To be fair, most of the people I worked with were rated as sevens and eights. There was even an occasional nine. I never awarded another ten.

That small gift that I hurriedly wrapped in a piece of foil and dropped into Janet's bag was, of course, a chocolate digestive biscuit.

8

The place wasn't the same after Janet had gone. The workload was certainly increased with one less dispenser, everything just seemed to be hard work. It was, as Doug commented on one of his visits, like swimming through treacle. I've never had the chance or indeed the wish to try that but we all knew what he meant. I looked forward to finishing my year under Archie's supervision. I would soon be able to register with the Pharmaceutical Society and be able to go 'flying solo' at last.

About a month before I finished, Mrs Moore went on holiday. Then Archie was called away for a special meeting with some of the other local managers and the TGM. Fortunately the meeting was fixed for a Wednesday which was always our quietest day.

Most of the shops on the high street closed for the half day at that time but the company had decreed just a few months earlier that we had to stay open all day. Doug wasn't available to cover Archie so an elderly, long retired ex-manager called Mr Ryeland was called in.

'He won't do much,' Archie explained. 'You and Amy will just have to cope as best you can. You'll be alright.' He looked a bit worried about leaving us but as all the other relief managers were occupied he didn't have much choice. There had to be a registered pharmacist on the premises for us to open at all.

Mr Ryeland arrived carrying his registration certificate with both hands. At that time all pharmacists had to display their certificate when on duty. Usually it was hung on the dispensary wall where the patients, who hadn't the faintest idea what it meant, were able to see it. It was meant to protect them from any unscrupulous people who might claim to be a pharmacist when in reality they are not. Displaying one's certificate when on duty was a legal requirement which pharmacists ignored at their peril.

Mr Ryeland's certificate, beautifully written in a majestic copperplate script, was encased in a magnificent but heavy wooden frame. Ormulu is a term which describes the gold coloured moulding used to decorate furniture and clocks. The word means, I believe, something like melted gold, and with its convoluted waves and swirls it does indeed look as though the item was covered in molten gold which when it cooled later, set solid to give those voluptuous shapes. You might expect to see a portrait framed in that style in a museum or stately home but it looked a bit over-the-top on the wall in our dispensary.

Old Mr Ryeland was a charming chap. He was long past his retirement age, rather out-of-date, and quite happy to leave everything to Amy and me. He sat himself down on a chair in the corner of the dispensary and, after we had checked each other's work, we placed the finished items in front of him for a final accuracy check.

'Fine, young man' he said to me each time, and, 'very nice, my dear,' to Amy.

He told us that he had several hobbies. He enjoyed gardening and photography but spent much of his time painting now he was retired. He used watercolours mostly, he said, but sometimes he painted in oils. He demonstrated his artistic ability by doodling scenes of us working on the sheets of white demi paper we used when weighing out the ingredients to make some mixture or other. He was really rather good, I thought, if more interested in Amy's figure than might be considered appropriate for a man of his age.

'I'd love to paint you in the nude one day,' he said to Amy, out of the blue. She glanced across at me, a horrified expression on her face. Those panda eyes had almost disappeared into her fringe. She was familiar, I'm sure, with most of the local lad's usual chat up lines but that threw her for a moment. She was, however, to prove equal to the challenge.

'OK,' she replied after taking a deep breath. 'But you'd better keep your socks on. This floor's very cold.'

Mr Ryeland had another great weakness, almost an addiction. He loved toffees and carried a paper bag full of them in his jacket pocket. He never once offered one to us, even to Amy. The company did, after all, ban us from eating or drinking in the dispensary. Clearly he thought that rule applied to us but not to him. Every so often Mr Ryeland would rummage in his pocket and produce a toffee. He always looked at it as if surprised to see such a thing then popped it into his mouth.

His false teeth were ancient and a pale yellow in colour and they seemed to move with a life of their own. I suppose his gums had shrunk as he got older and he hadn't bothered to replace the dentures. We couldn't look at him as he talked to us. Especially if he was chewing a toffee at the same time. There was always that feeling that the teeth would lose their battle to hang onto his gums and come flying out of his mouth.

He sat in the corner sucking and chewing his toffees until about mid-afternoon, then Amy suddenly grabbed my arm. I felt her nails dig into my skin and turned to see what she was up to.

I had heard the tap being turned on but there was nothing unusual in that. We often needed to measure out quantities of liquids and then we had to wash the measures as well as our hands at the dispensary sink.

Amy was staring at Mr Ryeland while digging her nails even further into my arm. I followed her eyes across the dispensary. He had taken out his dentures and stood at the sink trying to wash bits of toffee off them.

'Tea time,' I said quickly. 'Time for your break, Amy.' She stood fascinated, unable to move. 'Go on!' She ran out of the dispensary.

*

Mr Ryeland returned on the following Wednesday. Mrs Moore was still on holiday but Archie was due for some time off. Actually he hadn't had a break for about three weeks and looked really tired. When he found out that only Mr Ryeland was available to cover for him, he almost cancelled his day off.

'We'll be fine,' I said as he fretted the day before. 'Honestly. We can cope. It is a Wednesday again so it should be quiet. We managed all right last week.' Finally he agreed and confirmed his day off.

The day went as well as could be expected. Mr Ryeland doodled and watched Amy as we slaved away at the prescriptions. He ate a pound or two of toffees, mint flavoured we noticed this time, but refrained from rinsing his false teeth in the dispensary sink. As we approached five o'clock I thought we'd survived the day very well and was just congratulating myself when the telephone rang.

One of the many roles we carried out as pharmacists, at least until recently, is the supply of oxygen. We had several patients who for one reason or another needed to have a stock of oxygen in their homes. It was delivered to us in large cylinders which, as they were heavy, were usually delivered to the patient's home by Archie himself.

During my year in Barnsgrove he had trained me to deliver and set up the equipment so we shared the task between us. The kit consisted of the cylinder itself, a valve or regulator, a spanner to turn the flow of oxygen through the valve on and off and a face mask with a length of tubing and suitable connectors.

The call came from the panic-stricken wife of one of our patients. She had suddenly noticed that his last cylinder was almost empty and he was beginning to gasp for breath. Could we deliver one straight away? She had ordered another prescription from the surgery but it wouldn't be ready until tomorrow.

It seemed to me to be an emergency so I decided to take them a couple of cylinders immediately. I explained to Mr Ryeland and Amy that I would be going out and why.

'I'll try to be back before six o'clock,' I said to them. 'But you know how to lock up so if I'm longer than that, don't wait.' They nodded.

'What shall we do about the keys?' Amy asked. 'I'm off tomorrow.' I thought quickly.

'Lock up as normal then drop them through my letterbox at the flat as you go home please.' I hurried out to the store and collected a couple of oxygen cylingers, put them into my van and drove off.

I delivered and set up the oxygen cylinders. Normally I'd have gone straight back to work as it doesn't take long to swap the cylinders over when you've had a bit of practice. The patient was quite used to living with the equipment and we had been delivering the cylinders to him for a long time. I didn't need to explain their workings to him.

His chronic emphysema had been brought on by a lifelong addiction to cigarette smoking and probably not helped by his work in a foundry nearby. He had often been advised to stop smoking and claimed, between rasping coughs, to have cut down.

However, I could see the two packs of cigarettes on the shelf beside his chair and the butts in the fireplace. The walls and ceiling were stained brown as were his fingers and whole house smelled of smoke.

People who smoke always imagine that non-smokers can't tell. I knew that he was unlikely to change his ways but I repeated the advice about not smoking in that oxygen-enriched atmosphere of their living room.

'You'll blow yourself to kingdom come one day,' I said, repeating what I'd heard Archie say on many previous visits but he just smiled.

The elderly couple were very grateful for the speedy supply of the cylinders. The wife made us a nice cup of tea and brought out some homemade fruit cake. As her husband was still wheezing a bit, I stayed for a while until his breathing settled down. The cake was very nice too.

The shop keys were on my doormat when I got home. I usually parked my van at the back of the pharmacy overnight and had walked past the shop on my way home to my flat, trying the doors as I went. Everything looked secure so I relaxed for the evening.

The telephone rang in the middle of the night and woke me up. It was a duty sergeant at the local police station. I was listed as a key-holder for the pharmacy as I lived so close to the premises.

Dimly I heard the officer say that he had tried Mr John's number but there was no answer so he'd rung me. He said that one of his patrolling officers had reported that there was a light on upstairs at the back of the building.

'He's been all round the back of the pharmacy,' the officer said. 'There aren't any broken windows or signs of entry. The doors are secure. The alarm hasn't gone off. Just that light on. Do you want to have a look at it?'

From his description of the position of the lighted window I reckoned it was the staff toilet. I mentally balanced the thought of getting up, getting dressed and going to turn the light off against my warm bed and well-earned sleep.

'I'll bet somebody left the light on in the girl's loo,' I said. 'If the place looks secure otherwise I'll leave it until morning.' The police officer didn't seem too worried.

When arriving in the mornings we usually entered the building through the back door which faced into a yard where our deliveries arrived. I unlocked the door and went in, switching off the alarm as I did so.

My first task was to collect all the till floats and change bags from the safe in Archie's office so I switched the lights on and went up the stairs. In the office I found the safe door wide open and no money in sight. My heart stopped then sank, following my stomach down into my shoes.

'Christ!,' I said. 'Somebody did break in after all. They've taken all the money!'

I got down on my knees and scrabbled in the drawers in the bottom of the safe. We kept our most powerful drugs, morphine, diamorphine and so on, in those drawers at that time. Fortunately they were safely in place. The key was in the door of the safe. The intruder must have found it. It was a huge key, far too big to carry around so we always hid it in an empty canister among the hundreds of others on the dispensary shelf. No-one, we reckoned, would know that the apparently spare Amoxil canister held the key to the safe rather than hundreds of antibiotic capsules.

I knew that I had to phone the police. Explanations to Archie and head office would have to follow. That, I thought to myself, is the end of my career. All because I didn't bother to come and check out a possible break-in. Archie will never sign off my record of achievement now. I won't be able to register as a pharmacist. It was all a waste of time!

By now I was in a sweaty panic. I ran down the stairs and into the dispensary, flicking on the sales floor lights as I went. Had any of the drugs stored on the shelves in there been taken as well? I stopped and stared.

The till floats, bags of change and all the previous day's takings were carefully stacked along the dispensing bench. The money had been counted and each pile of notes and coins had its own little tally. There was a note complete with a little doodle from Mr Ryeland beside the cash.

'I'm afraid I didn't get chance to finish cashing up,' it said. 'I've left everything as tidy as I can for you to check.' He had signed it with a cheerful flourish. I have never ignored a call to any of the pharmacies I worked in since.

*

The last few weeks flew by. At last Archie could sign me off and I wrote a cheque for the necessary fee and posted it off. About ten days later my certificate arrived. It stated in a handsome script that I, Paul Frederick Rodgers was now registered as a Pharmaceutical Chemist and a member of The Pharmaceutical Society of Great Britain. A proud moment indeed. Then I had to pay another few pounds for a frame, just a simple one. No heavy ornate ormulu covered frame for me. I was showing it off to Mrs Moore and Amy when the telephone rang.

'Has your certificate arrived yet?' It was the secretary in the TGM's office. 'Yes? Thank heavens. The manager at the Saltwick branch has called in sick. Can you get there now?'

'My first proper job as a pharmacist,' I said as Archie shook my hand.

'No peace for the wicked. Best of luck,' he gripped my shoulder. 'Phone us if you get stuck with anything. Don't worry, that's no problem.'

*

It was about twelve miles to Saltwick and I arrived to find a very poorly looking manager sitting in the dispensary with his head in his hands. He was relieved to see help arrive and soon left to go home to bed.

'Babs'll look after you,' he said as he left. 'She'll lock up and take the keys home.'

Babs, short for Barbara I would think although no-one ever called her that, was a blond woman in her early forties. She didn't look to be in her forties mind you, but one of the girls in the shop told me that later. Also, I was told, she was not a natural blond. Women can be quite catty about their friends and colleagues sometimes.

The Saltwick branch must have been one of the smallest pharmacies in the company. It was one of those places that the company had gained when they took over another chain of pharmacies. The take over had been completed a couple of years earlier but the future of some of those pharmacies was still being determined.

Some of them were to be closed as they were near to the company's existing branches. Their stock and staff were to be amalgamated where possible. Some of the less profitable ones were sold off or just closed altogether.

The fate of the Saltwick branch still lay in the balance. It was too small really but there wasn't another pharmacy in the immediate area. I think the company was looking for a better site to relocate to but none had been found so far.

The whole shop was not much bigger than a decent sized living room. It looked like, and indeed was, the front room of a Victorian house. I found out later that an elderly lady lived alone in the rest of the property.

The dispensary was at the back of the room screened off from the rest of the shop floor by a shelf unit. A small counter and another series of shelves around the room completed the shop, or so I thought. There were just two members of staff other than Babs and the manager. One was a stout, mean-looking, forty-ish redheaded (not natural either I was told but could see that for myself) woman who tended to wear very bright red lipstick. She only worked in the mornings. The other, younger, slimmer and with a not unattractive smile, only worked in the afternoons.

They never, ever, worked together and in fact rarely met at all. However they argued all the time. Bitter messages and notes were passed back and forth. Each of them blamed the other if something wasn't done.

Often the one would say that she couldn't do something or other because the other one hadn't finished doing something else. I was only there for three days that week but I could have cheerfully rammed their heads together. Except of course they were never there at the same time for me to do so.

'Oh to be back in Barnsgrove,' I muttered to myself. It was not to be the last time I said or thought those words. I had begun to realise that I had had a very comfortable, well-supported existence there. 'Flying solo' brought many responsibilities as well as pleasures.

There were several people waiting for their medication when I arrived at the pharmacy so we hurried to complete their prescriptions. I checked the finished items, bagged them up and handed them out. As I returned to the dispensary I found a wooden barrier across the entrance.

'What are you doing?' I asked.

'I have to get something from the cellar,' Babs replied and crouched down to lift a large wooden hatch in the middle of the dispensary floor.' She disappeared down the steps and I heard her voice echo back. 'The barrier is to stop you falling down the hole if you don't look where you're going.'

It was an extraordinary sight. I have never seen another place like it. The whole pharmacy consisted of one room and a cellar. The cellar was the only storage space they had and that was known to flood occasionally after winter storms. I explored the cellar later while remembering the day I kissed Amy back in Barnsgrove.

9

During the eighteen months or so I spent working as a relief manager for the company, I was based at either Barnsgrove or Maythern but only actually worked in either of them a couple of times. It was nice to go back and have a gossip with the staff, I knew them all so well. I also went to the Greenlands branch to which Janet had been sent but sadly she'd left by then. Someone told me later that she had married David and moved away.

I was surprised with how little contact there was in those days between the staff of different branches. There could be two pharmacies a matter of a few miles apart but, apart from occasionally ringing up to check a price or borrow some stock, the staff, even the managers, rarely spoke to one another. They met even more rarely.

True, there were occasional manager's meetings but they were strictly business discussions, invariably dominated by the TGM. He did love the sound of his own voice. The branch staff never seemed to meet one another at all. Then one day, out of the blue, someone organised a cricket match for the managers and pharmacists of our district.

Archie flatly refused to have anything to do with the game and nominated me to go and represent the Barnsgrove branch. I happened to call in for a gossip on my day off, a thing I've learned never to do nowadays. You always get landed with doing something you'd rather not take on.

'How are you at cricket?' he demanded without warning.

'I haven't played since I was at school,' I replied. 'Even then it was only because I had to. I was never in a school team or anything. I played basketball though. I had an advantage there, being one of the tallest kids in my year.'

'Never mind,' he went on. 'I don't suppose any of the others have played for years either. This match is on the sports ground behind the village hall near The Lean branch. It starts at two o'clock on Sunday.' There was no question of me not playing, Archie had spoken.

The Lean branch was in one of the more expensive, desirable neighbourhoods on the edge of Birmingham. I often wondered why it was called "the lean", it seemed more like "millionaire's row" to me. A sort of inverted snobbery, I suppose. The Lean was where our TGM lived.

Sunday came bright and clear, also warm and dry. There was no chance that the game might be rained off. I didn't have anything like cricket whites in my wardrobe but then, with the exception of two other people, no-one else playing that day did either. Those two were the TGM himself and the manager of the largest branch in the city centre.

That manager was known as something of a poseur who had two other pharmacists working under him and lots of staff to do the real work. He and the TGM were two of a kind. I gather that is why they do what they do while we slave away at the coal face, as they say.

The rest of the players were a mixture of ages, sporting abilities and fitness, none of whom really wanted to be there. The only other face I knew was that of my old bird-watching friend, Pete Evans.

'Wotcher,' he said as we got ready for the match to begin. 'Seen any great tits lately?' This was his favourite greeting and he used it whenever we met. It wears a bit thin after a while, actually it wears a bit thin during the first time of hearing it.

The TGM and his chum picked their team first, taking anyone who looked at least capable of catching a ball. Pete and I ended up on what was obviously intended to be the losing team.

The TGM tossed a coin, won and decided to bat. He and the big shop manager walked casually out to take their guard. There was no umpire. The TGM's decision was likely to be final.

The pitch was normally used by a local cricket team and they had made a great effort to produce a good wicket as well as an excellent club house. It was all very picturesque and lovely to play on I'm sure. We didn't do it justice. All the care the club had taken was wasted on us. We were only there because we had to be there. The TGM had summoned us and we knew all too well that not to play would be a black mark against us in future.

Some of the older managers didn't care about that too much but we young newly hatched pharmacists were conscious of having to appear willing and eager to do anything we were asked to do in hope of a bit of promotion.

We of the opposing team spaced ourselves out around the pitch. No-one really took charge so there was no surprise when we realised we didn't have a bowler ready. A brief discussion ended with me taking the ball and preparing to bowl my first over in about five years, and to the TGM.

'Try not to hit him,' someone murmured as I began my run up. 'Unless you want another job.'

My first ball was a very slow full toss which was hit at some speed straight over the boundary for a six. The TGM had decided where the boundary was, by the way. He was the only person on the pitch who reckoned that the ball had bounced beyond the white line that marked the boundary. No-one cared to be the one to correct him.

My second ball was almost as bad as the first and the TGM leapt forward to repeat his shot. He didn't time it quite so well however and the ball rocketed straight towards Pete who was standing away to my right, halfway to the boundary.

'Catch!' we all shouted at him but unfortunately Pete had just then noticed a large bird circling over the trees at the end of the field. It was only a crow, even I knew that, but it fascinated him anyway. His gaze was up there with the bird when the ball hit him in his lower ribs. He collapsed with a groan. We offered no sympathy and left him lying on the grass to recover. The TGM went on to carry his bat through the whole innings, ending at 112 not out. We paused for tea.

I must say the tea was very nice, by far the best part of the day. Several of the manager's wives had come to watch our struggle and had brought a lovely selection of cakes and sandwiches. The posh end of the table had Thermos flasks of tea. Fortunately someone had thought to bring a few bottles of beer for the rest of us.

I sat with Pete and listened again to his tales about his adventures over shore and field in search of new birds. The smell of cut grass and the soft breeze cooling my brow soothed me and I relaxed. Cricket is all very well, I reckon, if you can just lie in the grass and watch it. I remembered a story Archie had told me about one of his old friends, Hughie Morgan, and repeated it to Pete.

Hugh worked part-time as a second pharmacist in one of the company's larger stores. He was nearing retirement at the time of this story and definitely had his eye on his final day. Then he would be able to forget work and concentrate on his other interests. One of these was a passion for cricket and particularly the Worcestershire County team.

The Australian touring team were due to play at the New Road ground in Worcester and Hugh had a ticket. He was looking forward to the game, one of the highlights of the season as far as he was concerned.

As Hugh was about to set off to the ground for the first day's play, his telephone rang. Another time he might have ignored it but on this occasion he didn't. He soon wished he had.

It was his boss, the manager at the store. Could Hugh work today? He, the boss, had an urgent meeting to attend. Hugh thought quickly then groaned and said he felt really awful, he'd picked up a stomach bug from somewhere. Hugh blamed the Chinese meal he had for his supper the previous evening. He'd spent most of the night in the bathroom, he moaned, and didn't think he'd be able to make it to the shop, sorry. He hung up and hurried away to get to the cricket ground before the start of play.

Hugh was enjoying the match. The day was warm but not too hot, he had a good view of the action and a pint of his favourite brew in his hand. The two sides were well matched and the excitement in the ground was growing by the minute.

Hugh felt someone brush past to get to the seats in the row behind him. He turned to scowl at the late arrival who had almost caused him to spill his drink. He found himself nose-to-nose with his manager from work.

They looked at each other for a moment. As Hugh had later explained, his manager shouldn't have been there either. He had persuaded someone else to cover for him even though it wasn't his day off.

The company was known to be particularly awkward about someone taking time off without permission especially as in this case it was just to watch a cricket match. The manager got up and moved to another seat, well away from Hugh. Nothing was ever said to Hugh and Hugh never mentioned the day to his boss.

We resumed play after tea but our hearts weren't in it. The TGM was in his element, altering the placement of his fielders from minute to minute and urging his team on to victory. I made one run and was then clean bowled. Pete was out first ball and none of our team scored double figures. We took defeat manfully and talked among ourselves of how a happy TGM is a good thing for all of us. Anyone listening to our comments might have imagined that we'd enjoyed the whole defeat.

*

Suddenly, the company decided on a complete reorganisation. Head office was still sorting out some of those pharmacies they had taken over, teams of people from head office were travelling around the country trying to implement the company's systems and attempting to incorporate the branches into various new regions and territories for administration.

At a stroke many of the pharmacies I had worked in so far disappeared into a new territory and I was sent to work in some of those that replaced them. I found that I enjoyed the variety of experiences gained by working in a different pharmacy each day. I had new people to chat to, exchange tall stories and jokes with or discuss the world's problems. It was still very rare that I met any of the other managers but I got to know their staff very well.

The first time I walked into the Mandley Green pharmacy I found a dispenser talking on the telephone in a foreign language. She seemed to be getting quite excited about something, waving her arms about as her voice rose. She was short, only about five foot tall, and very round. Almost as far round as she was high. I put my registration certificate down and looked around the dispensary.

It looked well organised, clean and tidy. The first impression was good. The dispenser, realising at last that I was there, barked a final word into the receiver and hung up. She turned and smiled, a simpering little girl smile and then she curtseyed to me. Yes, curtseyed!

I have a dream once in a while in which my staff line up to greet me as I arrive for work each day. They each bow or curtsey and I say "Good morning" as I pass. It will remain a dream I fear.

I said hello and introduced myself, we shook hands. She spoke with a thick central European accent and I strained to understand what she said.

'Good morning,' I understood that bit but then she lost me. 'I am Mrs Colitis,' Surely not I thought, but she went on. 'But that is a little difficult for people to understand so everybody calls me Mrs C.'

'Fair enough.' I said.

Mrs C, I was to learn, had arrived in England with her husband as a refugee during the Second World War. Before the war she had been a pharmacist in Latvia and her husband had been a highly qualified engineer. They arrived with almost nothing and thought they would be able to go home after the war was over. Then the Russians invaded her homeland, drove the Germans out but stayed to occupy the country. The Baltic States disappeared behind the Iron Curtain. Visitors were discouraged from going there and Mrs C lost touch with her friends.

'The Germans were bad enough but the Russians were much worse,' she told me one day. 'Until my country is free we cannot go home.'

There is a French Christmas carol called, I believe, "Mon Beau Sapin" which apparently translates as My Beautiful Fir (presumably Christmas) Tree. It is sung to the same or very similar tune as "The Red Flag" of communist Russia. A group of school children came one day just before Christmas that year to give a carol concert in the square outside the pharmacy. All went well until the youngsters began to sing that carol.

'Why are they singing that song,' Mrs C suddenly exploded. 'I hate that music, it isn't good music.'

She made to go out to stop the children singing but we managed to calm her down. I suppose if you see your country, your family and friends occupied as the Baltic States were, you have every reason to get so upset. Mrs C was very upset by the memories brought back by the sound of the music and cried for some time and I learnt a little more about the world.

As they had expected to go home when the war was over, neither Mrs C nor her husband had bothered to seek work in their previous fields. They would have had to re-qualify in their old professions and learn about the British ways of working. Each of them had therefore taken a job as a temporary measure. He was a groundsman for the local council and she worked in a factory at first then joined the company as a dispenser. They had managed to save enough to buy a small house and raise a family. When I worked with her nearly thirty years after the end of the war they were still hoping to go home one day.

The Mandley Green branch was another of those small, cramped places, like the one at Saltwick but this time someone at head office had decided that it should close. There were two other company branches nearby and they were in much larger, more modern premises.

The manager who had run Mandley for several years was moved to another branch and I was instructed to cover the day-to-day running of the place until all the stock had been finally removed. The staff were to be transferred to another branch unless they decided to leave.

The Mandley branch was about fifty miles from my flat so, as this closing down process was only supposed to take about three weeks, I drove back and forth from Barnsgrove each day. Nearly two months later the company, in its wisdom, suddenly announced that they had decided to keep the pharmacy open after all and I was appointed to be the new manager. I started looking for another flat.

Two of the staff from the shop had already been transferred to another branch and they decided to stay where they were. Quite typically, I was only allowed to take on one new girl to replace the two of them. I advertised the job and began to interview the applicants.

This was my first attempt at interviewing staff but there was really only one person suitable so the choice was easy to make. She was a young Asian woman born in Sri Lanka but brought up in Uganda. Her family came to England to avoid the growing hostility that they received from the Ugandan authorities. Her name was long and, to us, unpronounceable but she loved the English girl's names.

'Please call me Becky,' she had said on her first day.

Her English was very good, with just a slight accent. Mrs C had more trouble understanding her than the rest of us. A few days after Becky started work in the pharmacy, Mrs C cornered me in the stockroom. She looked troubled and as usual when excited over something or other, her accent became more difficult to understand.

'Do you think it is really alright for us to call her Blacky?' she hissed in what she imagined was a whisper. Becky laughed the loudest of us all.

*

At that time we used a laundry service which came each week to collect our dirty towels, particularly the tea-towels from the dispensary, and supply fresh clean ones in their place. This system had been used for many years but, in their wisdom, head office cancelled it. They decided that it was cheaper to supply rolls of disposable paper towels instead of paying for the laundry.

Mrs C was aghast. I suppose she had seen some terrible deprivations during her time as a refugee and the thought of ripping off pieces of paper, using them once then throwing them away was too much for her to contemplate.

She started taking the old tea-towels home to wash and then began to collect up all the not-too-wet sheets of paper we'd thrown away. I didn't realise what she was doing at first until, one day, I reached under the dispensary workbench for a box of dressings and found a huge wad of slightly damp paper towels resting on top of the fridge. She was trying to use the heat from the back of the fridge to dry the paper towels so they could be used again.

It took quite some persuading to get her to stop doing this. Waste of any sort is wrong of course. I have often thought Mrs C would be in her element in these day when we try to recycle everything. Perhaps she was right after all.

Mrs C retired about two years after I started working at the Mandley Green branch. Her husband had also retired and they spent their days gardening and visiting their grown up children and many friends in the area. Whenever I saw them they invariably told me about their dream to go back home one day. They had enquired about visiting their homeland, just for a holiday, but had been advised that the authorities there would never allow it.

Just before I left to move on to my next appointment I went to see them. We sat in their garden, eating peaches picked from their tree and drinking wine as they told me of their plans to visit friends in South Africa. They both died, around the same time, a few years later. They never got back to Latvia. Sadly they died just before the Berlin Wall came down, before the opening up of the old Eastern Bloc countries and before their homeland became independent. They could go back now, I expect, but it is far too late.

10

After hearing Mrs C's story of their escape to England during the war, I felt very fortunate to have grown up and to continue to live in a country like Britain. I have not had to fight or kill to protect my home, hide in bomb shelters or suffer starvation and ethnic cleansing. There are terrible terrorist attacks in our cities nowadays and we must be vigilant of course but by and large this is a safe country to live in.

I never had to experience anything like what Mrs C and thousands of other people all over the world have had to suffer. I suppose I'd have to cope with it but they have my admiration. Often we have no idea of the struggles that some people have had to endure to protect their families and homes or just to exist.

A young man came into the pharmacy one morning to enquire about the possibility of a temporary job. He was about to leave school and had been accepted to go up to university to study pharmacy.

During the summer holidays in the previous year he had worked in a hospital pharmacy and now wanted to spend a few weeks in the retail branch of the profession to gain some actual experience. He wanted to compare the two branches of our professions, quite wisely I thought.

I had to get permission from head office but eventually they agreed to pay him a small wage until he started his pharmacy course at university. Konstantine, or Dino as he preferred, was the son of a Greek-Cypriot family. They ran a small restaurant not far from the pharmacy. His mother turned out to be one of our regular customers, often calling into the pharmacy to collect medicines for the family.

Dino was a lovely chap, highly intelligent and keen to learn about pharmacy. He had many questions which I tried to answer and he explained that his ambition was eventually to return to Cyprus and have his own pharmacy. He had an uncle who owned a pharmacy in Paphos and Dino wanted to do the same. They might, he suggested, eventually end up with a chain of pharmacies just like our own dear company all over the island. With his enthusiasm I didn't doubt that he would succeed.

In the meantime I was invited to have a meal at the restaurant with the family. I hadn't eaten there before but soon became a great fan of Dino's Mother's cooking. I was a slim chap at the time and Dino's mother didn't think I ate enough. She piled my plate higher each time I returned and while I sometimes struggled to eat it all the food was wonderful.

Back in the 1970's foreign food was, to me at least, well, foreign. I had been abroad only a couple of times and then only to France and once to Switzerland on a school skiing trip. With Dino's family I sampled souvlakia, kleftiko, keftedhes, sheftalia and much more.

The desserts were full of syrup or honey. I ate baklava, daktila and, my favourite, soujoukkos. I learned not to call the gelatin cubes prepared with rose water and dusted with powdered sugar Turkish Delight. Like many Greeks they hated the Turks. The delicious sweets were known as loukoumia to the Greek Cypriots.

Dino and his family told me stories about their island, known as Aphrodite's birthplace, and introduced me to Cypriot wine. I wasn't a wine drinker really and hadn't even realised that they made wine in Cyprus but the family had friends who sent or brought bottles to them.

I was invited into their living room after dinner one evening. It was a comfortable place and with a full stomach I settled down on the sofa with a cup of coffee. On the sideboard opposite my seat was a large photograph in an ornate silver frame. The subject of the photograph was a young man, handsome with a small moustache and a far-away look in his eyes. Dino's father noticed my interest.

'That is a photograph of Evagoras Pallikarides,' he said then seeing my blank look added. 'My family lived in the same village as his mother in Cyprus. The village is called Tsada, it is near Paphos. I knew him when he was child.'

'A handsome young man,' I said.

'He was hanged by the British,' he said quietly and I noticed tears in his eyes. 'A hero in our fight for independence.' He touched the frame gently then sat down to tell me the story.

I had quite enjoyed history at school although in my day it consisted mainly of lists. Lists of dates, of kings and queens and of battles, learned by heart. We only covered British history and touched on parts of the old Empire. Even European history was only mentioned where there was a British connection and our syllabus ended where the First World War started.

I am ashamed to say that I knew nothing about the events he described that took place in Cyprus. I don't think I'm alone in that. Thousands of people take a holiday in Cyprus these days. Many Britons have bought flats or villas there so that they can spend some time away from our miserable winters and share holidays with family and friends. I have been to that beautiful island myself since that evening.

Few, if any, of those holidaymakers would know about the terrible civil war of the 1950's. Perhaps even fewer would bother to find out. Dino's father told me his story and later I looked up further details of the terrible times. It was what some people have called a "small war" but still an awful period in British history.

Cyprus was a British colony in the 1950s, used as a base to cover the eastern end of the Mediterranean and the northern end of the Suez Canal. The population of the island at the time was about 80 per cent Greek-Cypriot and most of the rest were of Turkish origin.

Nowadays the Chloraka coast near Paphos is a popular holiday destination, lined by a wall of hotels, bars and restaurants. In the early 1950s it was a deserted coastline remote from the central administration in Nicosia. There, in November 1954, Georgios Grivas landed with the first shipment of arms brought from Greece via Rhodes by fishing boat.

Grivas was a Cypriot-born colonel in the Greek army who was to adopt the name Dighenis after a Byzantine epic hero. He was known to be austere, very right wing and fanatically anti-Turk. His aim was to gain independence from the British and to achieve union, what he called Enosis, with Greece.

Grivas had organised and directed cells of the EOKA organisation while Archbishop Makarios III became the spiritual and political head of the organisation. EOKA stood for Ethniki Organosis Kyprion Agoniston. To Grivas they were freedom fighters, to the British they were terrorists.

The first bombs exploded on the first of April 1955. Like all terrorist campaigns, success depended on provoking fear and distrust between communities of ordinary people and also on the recruitment of idealistic young people to their cause.

Reports of casualties began to rise. Uniformed policemen and British soldiers were the targets along with anyone suspected of being an informant. Undoubtedly the temptation was also there to get rid of anyone you didn't like or owed money to. Ledra Street in the island's capital Nicosia became known as Murder Mile after so many assassinations took place there.

The military took over from the civil administration and a state of emergency was declared. Public assemblies were banned, strikes became illegal and the death penalty was introduced for carrying weapons.

The Pancyprian Gymnasium, a prestigious academy for Greek-Cypriot students in Nicosia, was a hotbed of support for Enosis. Grivas has studied there and many of his freedom fighters were recruited from this establishment.

At first the students daubed slogans, removed British flags, took part in marches and demonstrations but some were drawn into EOKA itself just as young people are recruited as suicide bombers or terrorists today. They would be prepared die to further their master's ambitions.

Evagoras Pallikarides was one such youth. He was a final year student at the academy and took part in some of the demonstrations. Then he joined EOKA and took part in their attacks on police stations, British personnel and camps.

The promotion of fear and distrust continued, there were massacres in both Greek and Turkish communities. A British army sergeant was shot dead on Murder Mile while walking with his 2-year old son, a soldier's wife was killed, another injured.

The period claimed, the records show, the lives of 104 British military personnel and policemen (British, Greek-Cypriot and Turkish), 84 Turkish civilians and 366 Greek-Cypriots. It was estimated that of those 366 Greek-Cypriots, about 200 were killed by EOKA for opposing their cause. Truly, a dirty war.

Eventually a ceasefire was announced and, following a United Nations resolution, Cyprus became independent with Archbishop Makarios appointed as the first president. The union with Greece was explicitly forbidden.

Grivas fought to gain Enosis again in 1971. He returned to the island to form EOKA-B. He had much less support this time. By now Greece itself was governed by a military junta and the Cypriots did not want to exchange their newly won independence from Britain for a future of being ruled by a dictatorship in Athens. The attempted coup failed but the unrest resulted in the Turkish army invading the north of the island.

Indiscriminate killings and ethnic cleansing continued until all the Greek-Cyriots moved to the southern end of the island and all the Turks to the north. Friends were divided, homes and businesses abandoned. Some of the deserted villages can still be seen, weed filled collapsing homes in ghost villages. A line was drawn on the map in green ink between the two communities. This, the Green Line, is patrolled by the United Nations forces and remains in place today.

'Evagoras Pallikarides was captured while moving arms and equipment between one hideout and another.' Dino's father explained in the hushed room. 'His trial took place in February 1957. The death penalty had been introduced for anyone carrying weapons and he was sent to the gallows in March 1957. He was just 19 years old.'

Dino's mother lifted the portrait, turned over the frame and passed it to me to read the words written on the back of the photograph.

'This is a copy of the words he wrote to his friends before he was hanged, ' she said and translated them for me.

"At this time one among you is missing. One who has gone in search of some fresh air. One whom you may never see alive again. Do not weep on his grave. Do not mourn for him. Only scatter a few May flowers on his grave. That is enough for him.

I will take an uphill path
I will scale the mountains
I will find the blessed steps
That will lead to freedom."

I looked at Dino. He was about the same age as that idealistic young man had been at his death. I thought what a waste it was that young people were, and still are, taken from their families and turned into killers just to further another person's ambition to gain power and influence. And I thought about the British personnel who also died, far from home, trying to keep the peace.

'When will we ever learn?' I murmured more to myself than anyone else.

Dino's father leaned across and gripped my hand. 'It was a long time ago and we must forgive, but we won't forget him.'

11

My next appointment was to be as the manager of the company's Kemston branch. It was a modest step up the promotion ladder, a larger and busier pharmacy than the Mandley Green branch. I had worked there before as a relief manager when I was based in Barnsgrove and was pleased to be moving back to the area. About 35 miles from Barnsgrove itself, Kemston is set in the lovely countryside that makes up the counties we know as the Marches, the boundary between England and Wales.

One of my first tasks was to find a new home. By this time I wanted a place of my own, maybe a little way out of town, to settle down and stay for a few years. My salary had risen with the new position and I began to feel more secure, at least in the financial sense.

The Marches, near the border with Wales is still a relatively unspoiled rural landscape. There are few motorways or theme parks, just fertile, sheltered farmland. The local tourism people call it "the land that time forgot" and you can still wander among half timbered villages and small market towns, along narrow country lanes with hedge-lined fields and orchards. I collected a pile of brochures from the local estate agents and began my search for a new home.

House prices in the late 1970s were much less than they are now of course. However, they seemed steep to me at the time.

I saw a lot of very nice houses and had many sleepless nights afterwards wondering how on earth I would ever pay for one of them. It sounds so stupid now when such a place would cost £200,000 plus and you'd pay £12,000 for a half decent car. You could get a nice house for £12,000 in the 1970's

Exploring the country lanes around Kemston was a lovely way to spend a day off or a summer evening. The countryside appeared to be full of old pubs, sheep, cattle and cider apple orchards. I discovered Westons Stowford Press cider and was often diverted from my house search in order to follow the course of one or other of the local rivers, the Arrow, the Lugg, the Teme and of course the Wye and the Severn. All of these rivers were beautiful, unspoiled peaceful waterways surrounded by ancient villages, castles and medieval churches.

At last I had to buckle down to some serious house-hunting and compiled a short list from that pile of brochures. Top of my list was a small bungalow set within a lovely garden. A brook ran through the bottom of the garden, a kingfisher had flown along just above the surface of the water on my first visit.

The view from the bungalow was heavenly. One could look across a small valley of fields, woods, hedges and see the distant hills of the Welsh border in the background. There was a farm down the lane and apple orchards in the fields behind the bungalow. A flock of friendly sheep lived among the apple trees.

I went to see the place three times and felt it got better each time. My last visit was on a lovely Sunday afternoon. It looked idyllic, and the asking price was just on the limit I'd set myself for the mortgage. It was time to make a decision. I spent the rest of the weekend worrying about the money then went into work on Monday morning.

Trying to put the decision out of my mind I worked hard until just before lunchtime. I had made up my mind to make an offer for the bungalow and was just reaching for the telephone when someone tapped on the counter to get my attention.

'Hello, Mr Rodgers, I presume,' he said. 'I bet you don't remember me,' A man with a vaguely familiar face stood in front of the counter. I thought quickly, he looked familiar, I should know him. The penny dropped at last.

'You're the chap who brought me a sack of potatoes after we'd dispensed your wife's prescription. It was after work on a Saturday. In Barnsgrove.' I shook his hand.

'Well done,' he smiled. 'We moved out this way a couple of months ago. The old farm was sold, we were only tenants there and had no choice but to move out. The fields round that farm are going to be built over now but I had the chance to take over a place near Middleton. Its not far from here, about three miles out of town.'

'Yes, I was out that way yesterday,' I said. 'Looking at a nice bungalow. I'm thinking of buying something like that, it was just right.'

'I saw you there when I was working in one of my fields,' he said. 'We've got the farm further down the lane. I thought I recognised you in the distance and then I had a better view of you as you drove away. That's why I've come in to see you.

'That is a nice enough bungalow alright but I didn't know if you had been told about the plan to build a large turkey breeding unit in the field opposite. I thought you should know about that.

'The people selling the place are desperate to get away before the work starts. The smell alone from those places can be awful. Then there's all the lorries coming and going and the manure they produce. That gets spread on the fields you know. Its very useful but it stinks something terrible.'

'No-one mentioned that,' I said.

'Maybe you would have found out before you handed over any of your cash,' he said with a troubled look. 'But then maybe you wouldn't. I didn't want you to be messed about. I'm still grateful for what you did for us that day. My wife was really ill, that medicine saved her life, I reckon.'

'Well thank you,' I shook his hand again feeling relieved that I hadn't made that phone call yet.

'One good turn deserves another,' he answered.

*

I found my house in the end. It is quite small and in a village about seven miles from the nearest market town. I moved in over the August Bank Holiday and after decorating the place to my taste, the Laura Ashley wallpaper went for a start, I reflected on the name of the house. For many years it had been owned by a lady who had now moved into a flat to be near her daughter's home in town. The house was known as "Pansy Cottage". Well I couldn't have that so a new name was invented.

Several years before that time I had been interviewed by an area manager. It was an early form of annual appraisal, I suppose, although neither of us understood what we were supposed to be doing. At one stage he asked me what I wanted to do in the future. I think now that he meant me to say what I'd be doing within the company. Unfortunately the company was losing its appeal at that time and I rambled on for a while about my ideas of a life outside pharmacy instead.

'I'd really like to be able to just footle around the world,' I had said as he gazed into space. 'You know, nothing planned or definite. Not too much in the way of responsibility. Just to find lots of interesting things to learn and to do, new places to explore and new people to meet without getting too deeply involved in anything specific.'

Eventually, his eyes swivelled back to meet mine and I realised that he didn't understand a word I'd said. I made up some nonsense about working to improve the branch and build up our customer base and so on but both of us had lost heart with the interview. Later I looked up the word footle in a dictionary. It means to loiter aimlessly. That is still my secret ambition. When I grow up I want to be a footler.

Where, I asked myself would a footler live? What cosy spot would a footler use to hide away from all the stress at work and similar problems? A nook of course! Or possibly a cranny. So the name of my house was changed to "Footler's Nook" and so it is to this day.

*

Having worked five or six days a week and possibly had to turn out for an hour of rota service on the Sunday, one appreciates any time off. In a small town like Kemston my regular customers soon knew as much about me as I knew myself.

Many of them knew where I lived and what my everyday habits were. Its not that they are nosey, although some of them might be thought to take an unhealthy interest in their neighbours. It is just the way it is in such places.

Occasionally I found a customer on my doorstep at home wanting a prescription dispensed or just to ask a question. Generally speaking I didn't mind too much although when a chap hammered on my door at seven o'clock one Christmas Day morning to complain that he couldn't get the camera he bought in the pharmacy to work, I may not have been my usual cheerful self. Especially when I pointed out that he had put the batteries in the wrong way round!

On the other hand, sometimes I really don't mind. There was a doctor in Kemston during the time I worked there named Williamson. He was getting on in years and should quite reasonably be thinking in terms of retirement. Dr Williamson was one of the rare breed of doctors, still rarer these days, who worked alone. In fact, after the story of the infamous Dr Harold Shipman came to light the whole concept of single-handed doctor practices was discouraged. Far better to have several doctors working under one roof. That way they can keep an eye on one another!

A one-man practice meant that he was almost permanently on call. He would have had to employ a locum to cover him if he wanted a holiday but I don't remember him not being there while I lived in the area. He loved his patients and had followed their lives and, in many cases, their parent's and grandparent's lives through his long career.

Once in a while he would be called out in the evening or on a Sunday to a patient who needed an urgent supply of, say, antibiotics or painkillers. He always carried a small stock of medicines for a range of conditions in his bag and so would be able to supply enough for his patient to start a course of treatment. He would give them a prescription for any following doses which could then be dispensed when the pharmacy was open. Sometimes he found that he needed to prescribe something he didn't normally carry with him. After all there is a limit to what he could fit in a doctor's bag.

On some of these occasions he would turn up at my house, apologise for troubling me then insist on driving me down to the pharmacy. I would dispense his prescriptions and we'd have a little chat about the state of the world as he drove me back home. He would then deliver the medication to his patient himself. You won't find many doctors like him nowadays.

I had taken the opportunity to get a lie-in one Sunday morning, then wandered slowly down to the kitchen to get a cup of tea. A movement out in the garden caught my eye. Someone was sitting on a chair in the garden, my garden. He had his feet up on a low wall and appeared to be enjoying the sunshine and sniffing my flowers.

I opened the door, wondering who the devil he was. Hearing the door open the figure turned round. Dr Williamson smiled his calm friendly smile. He hadn't wanted to disturb me, he said. He'd realised I was having a lie in and hoped he hadn't cut it short but would I mind coming to dispense a prescription for him. He was such a lovely man and only ever disturbed me, as he put it, when absolutely necessary, so off we went.

Sometimes one really doesn't mind being disturbed at all. One lovely summer evening I had wandered down the lane for a walk. I spent quite a long time leaning over a stone bridge just staring down into the brook that ran beneath. A small family of water voles were paddling around, feeding, while the youngsters kept bumping into one another. I'm certain they must have been playing at being little furry wet dodgem cars. The birds were singing in soothing tones and my mind began to relax after the hectic day.

I could hear a farmer working in one of the fields beyond the crab apple trees in the hedge, the cows and sheep were settling down for the night and only a few other people passed by on bicycles or on foot. One girl went by on horseback while singing quietly to herself.

My walk stretched out for much longer than I had intended. I had spent quite some time watching a flock of swifts screaming high above while taking a last feed of midges and the sun had gone down behind the distant shadowy hills by the time I turned back for home..

It was getting quite dark when I eventually paused near my gate. It was even darker under the trees, and I listened to an owl in the wood. There were bats flitting across my garden, between my new apple trees. A car pulled up behind me in the lane and the driver's window was slowly wound down. A soft, husky woman's voice drifted out into the warm evening.

'Is that you Mr Rodgers?' she said, seductively in my imagination at least.

'Yes,' I replied trying to make out who it was in the dark interior of the car. I didn't recognise the voice. She sounded very nice though, about my age I thought, and a most attractive shape as far as I could see. I began to wonder if she might like a glass of wine or something and was about to ask her in.

'Good,' she murmured in that same husky voice. 'I hoped I would find you in.'

'Oh yes. I'm definitely in.'

'I'm staying with my brother, John Murray,' she explained, suddenly brisk and businesslike. 'In Eltnan Street. He is one of your patients.' I nodded uselessly in the dark. 'His asthma is playing up badly tonight and he sent me to ask if you would dispense this prescription for him. He needs the inhalers.'

Well I sighed, then fetched my car and followed her into town. I opened up the pharmacy and dispensed the inhalers. It was an emergency, I told myself, and she would be grateful for my help. I let her out of the shop and turned to lock the door.

By the time I had finished and turned back to speak to her again, she had got back into her car. She waved cheerfully and called "thank you!" as she drove off and disappeared into the night. I stared after her for a moment or two then drove home.

The next day I noticed that the prescription had been written out by the doctor almost a week earlier. John Murray could have collected his medication in plenty of time and had it all ready at home in case of an attack.

'Inconsiderate beggar! There was no need to drag me out at night,' I muttered to myself, then remembered the delicious feeling I had when hearing that seductive voice coming out of the darkness. Perhaps it was worth it to be disturbed after all. Sometimes I really didn't mind being troubled.

12

There are something like 10,000 pharmacies in Britain. You will find one in most high streets, many shopping centres, sometimes attached to doctor's surgeries, tucked away in the corners of supermarkets, on railway stations, in airports and even sometimes at pop concerts and sporting occasions. The work in all of them has many similarities.

A prescription which is dispensed in a pharmacy in a tiny pharmacy on the outskirts of Manchester will be dealt with in just the same way as one in a pharmacy in a huge supermarket in Newcastle or Southampton. The stock will quite possibly have been delivered through the same wholesaler system, the dispenser was trained in much the same way and the paperwork will be exactly the same. The paperwork is the bit the patient rarely gets to see. You do not want to see it.

Just as all pharmacies have many similarities in what they do, there are also some differences. At the Kemston pharmacy I found that we dispensed a lot of items you might not think of as medicines at all. We supplied more dressings, incontinence requirements and supplies for stoma therapy than I had ever done in other pharmacies.

Each month the Department of Health sends an updated copy of a book called the Drug Tariff to every doctor's surgery and pharmacy in the land. Incidentally, I reckon we could discontinue sleeping tablets altogether if they would allow us to dispense a few pages of this book instead. Just reading the first three pages puts me to sleep every time. It would save the NHS a fortune.

The Drug Tariff is a very precise (some might say pedantic) list of drugs, the prices that the NHS will pay for them, specifications for all those appliances like trusses and hosiery, information about oxygen supply, the details of every dressing allowed on the NHS and pages and pages of stoma and incontinence supplies. It also lists what we call "blacklisted medicines" which the NHS will not pay for at all.

As these details can change from one month to the next, the wise pharmacist and dispenser will keep the Drug Tariff close at hand. I spent more time at Kemston perusing the information in that book than I ever have before or since.

For example, a manufacturer may produce a whole range of dressings and several sizes of each of them. The Drug Tariff might only list and therefore allow us to dispense, a few certain sizes. That might easily have changed by next month. We have to know which ones are allowed.

Then there was the farce about quantities. Sometimes a doctor or nurse will write a prescription for dressings and just specify "one pack" or even abbreviate that to "OP" thinking that we will supply a pack of them. The NHS in its wisdom decided that the figure 1, the words one pack or "OP" all meant just one dressing. Just the one single solitary dressing. What, you might wonder, is the point of one dressing. Surely they have to be changed? We spent hours getting prescriptions altered by the doctors and nurses to comply with the Drug Tariff requirements

Often we had the same sort of problem with incontinence supplies. These include catheters and drainage bags of various sorts. Dozens and dozens of different ones are listed in the Drug Tariff and therefore we are allowed to dispense them, but there are others which are not.

Only if they are clearly identified in the current month's Drug Tariff will the NHS allow us to supply them. The prescription had to be written very precisely or the NHS just wouldn't accept it. The onus is on the pharmacy staff to make sure the cost of the appliances being paid for by the Department of Health is for the correct item.

The same problem applies with the items needed for stoma patients. There are dozens of different types of bags for colostomy or ileostomy patients. The patient has to have the correct one or it will not fit the stoma. The prescription has to describe exactly the right one or the NHS will reject it. Then the pharmacy itself would have to bear the cost of whatever had been supplied in good faith to the patient and many dressings and most stoma supplies are much more expensive than any patient might imagine. Forty or fifty pounds a time is not unusual.

A colostomy is a surgical procedure where the large bowel or colon is diverted to open out onto the surface of the abdomen. It is a surprisingly common operation and most pharmacies will have a few such patients. The patient's faeces don't go through the rectum to be excreted as usual but are collected in a bag attached via a flange to the surface of the skin.

The colostomy may be permanent as when, for example, a large amount of the bowel is removed because of cancer, or it may be a temporary arrangement perhaps to give part of the bowel time to recover after an operation. Generally the bag will fill twice a day and it has to be replaced after each bowel movement.

An ileostomy is a similar operation but involves the ileum, the lowest part of the small intestine. Again the contents of the small bowel are collected in a disposable bag attached to the surface of the abdomen. As ileostomies are usually permanent, the patient will need a supply of the correct bags for the rest of his or her life.

Along with the bags we dispense all sorts of wipes, flanges and deodorants as listed in the Drug Tariff. There are hundreds of items which can be dispensed and no pharmacy can possibly stock them all so it is usually necessary to order what is wanted for each prescription. Patients are strongly advised to get their prescription into the pharmacy in plenty of time.

Patients tend to blame us if we can't dispense a prescription straightaway as they demand. The reason often is that the prescription isn't written out properly and we just can't do it. Even if we can get confirmation over the telephone as to what is required we still have to get the prescriber to give us the correct prescription.

The whole business puts a lot of strain on the dispensing staff. They want to get on with the dispensing as much as the patient, but so much of their time is spent chasing up incomplete prescription forms or trying to clarify what is wanted and getting the prescriptions amended.

Many doctors, some nurses and most of their receptionists and secretaries do not have a clue about writing prescriptions for dressings and other appliances. Many of these people think they know everything of course and some of them can be irritatingly smug. In fact there is an old but sadly relevant joke in pharmacy which goes; what is the difference between a doctor and God? The answer is; God doesn't think He is a doctor.

*

Writing prescriptions is but one part of a doctor's work, of course. Most of them are very caring and professional people. I'm sure most of us will be grateful for their services at one time or another. However the prescription writing part of their work is the part that impacts most on pharmacists and their dispensers. Unless the prescribers do their part of the job properly we can't even begin to do ours at all and some doctors can be less than helpful.

'Here's my prescription,' a vinegar-faced woman wearing a thick coat the precise colour of acute diarrhoea, wellington boots and a deerstalker hat thrust her form into my hands. 'It's only a few pills. I'll wait. I'm in a hurry.'

I read the prescription, or at least I tried to read it. My dispenser looked over my shoulder and shook her head as well. It was one of those prescriptions we dreaded. A handwritten one issued by Dr Tweedy from the practice over the road.

'I'm sorry,' I said. 'I can't read it.'

'Don't be stupid!' she snarled. 'Just get on with it. You're supposed to be the chemist! What do you mean you can't read it? Hurry up I haven't got all day.'

'I really can't read it,' I said and turned the form round to show her. I pointed at the wriggling squiggles that decorated the spaces at the top of the form. 'You try. What does that say?'

She glared at me, then at my dispenser and snatched the form back and stared at it.

'Well! I don't know! You're supposed to be the expert,' she threw the form down on the counter again.

'That is supposed to be your name and address,' I said as calmly as I could. 'You can't read that even though you know what it is meant to say. What chance do you think I've got? I don't know you at all. Also I can't read what he's prescribed for you. The rest of the form is a meaningless scribble.'

'What are you going to do about it?' she demanded.

'I'll try to find out what it says but it may take some time.'

'Don't take too long about it!' she grunted.

I phoned the surgery at once but the receptionist told me that Dr Tweedy had just gone out. Doctor's handwriting is seen as a joke to many people but this particular doctor had the worst writing I have ever seen in my forty years and he thought it was so terribly funny that no-one could read it.

The idiot probably never had a clue how many times his patients nearly ended up with the wrong medication because of his inconsiderate behaviour. His writing was not just bad but sometimes he actually managed to make one drug name look near enough to a different one to make us think we actually knew what he wanted.

We always double checked his prescribing. Quite probably he and his long-suffering partners and receptionists thought we were being awkward but we had to make sure the patient received the correct medication every time.

Dr Tweedy had gone out, the receptionist said. She had hesitated and sounded annoyed. We knew, as did his partners and receptionists that Dr Tweedy often "went out" during surgery hours. His usual habit was to drape his stethoscope around his neck then rush out through the waiting room saying to anyone still waiting that he had to go to an emergency.

Perhaps once in a while an emergency might occur but we all knew he was off home early. He'd done what he considered enough work for the day and he was off.

Unless another doctor happened to be free Dr Tweedy's patients would be told to make another appointment. Heaven only knows why his long-suffering patients, his partners, or indeed the local health authority, put up with him.

13

Within the organisation of the Royal Pharmaceutical Society there is a system of local branches which cover areas that in many cases fit neatly with the counties. The branch system is supposed to provide a means by which pharmacists in a particular area can meet to talk over their mutual problems, exchange ideas and pass on any vital information they need. No matter whether the pharmacist works in a hospital or a high street pharmacy, for any company or is self employed, retired or part time or in the midst of a full time career, all are welcome.

Now that I had settled in Kemston, I decided to attend one of the branch meetings to get to meet some of my new colleagues. They all seemed very nice although I was surprised that there were so few of them present. Someone explained that although there were about 80 registered pharmacists living within the area covered by the branch, most of them had either retired or didn't work in pharmacy anymore.

'We usually get about a dozen or so members to our meetings,' I was told. 'That's apparently about an average percentage of participants in most branches. Usually it's the same people who come each time.'

Many of the local branch meetings were organised with a speaker to talk to us about some aspect of our work and I found some of them most interesting. Sometimes a buffet was included as well. Strangely, those meeting were much better attended than those without refreshments. However once in a while the committee booked an evening trip out somewhere in the hope of attracting a few more pharmacists to participate.

One such evening, in mid October of that year, was spent with a cider producer deep in the lush Herefordshire countryside. It was very educational and up to a point I found the evening very enjoyable too.

Brewing beer, even of real ales, we were told, can take place all year round but the best cider is made when the fruit is ripe. The month of October, we were pleased to find, is that time of the year. The time when the process begins. The ripe apples are collected in the local orchards and taken to the producer. Many mornings I followed slow tractors pulling overloaded trailers piled high with fruit which delayed my journey to work but I reckon the resulting drinks made that worth while.

Most producers use a mixture of apple varieties. We were introduced to Redstreak, Kingstone Black and several other names that must have survived for centuries. We heard about varieties with strange names like Hangdown and Slack-my-girdle but didn't get chance to taste the cider made from them.

Our guide told us that cider had been known since biblical times. It was called shekh'ar in the bible. The ancient Greeks and Romans made the stuff as did the Anglo-Saxons.

Cider is also said to be good for us, a rich source of antioxidants, when drunk in sensible units. We followed the process with avid interest and were pleased to find ourselves ending the tour in the inn next door to the brewery. Some tasting was in order.

The meeting had proved to be a popular one. Many more pharmacists had arrived than they'd expected. I think that tells you something about pharmacists. They do want to learn and stay up to date in their work but after the pharmacy closes they would rather relax with a pint than be lectured in what they should be doing. These social evenings were much more popular than the educational talks.

Among the crowd I'd spotted a face from my past. We greeted each other and walked round the tour together but didn't have chance to chat until we sat down in the pub afterwards. Will was about my age, we'd both studied at Aston University and had some mutual friends.

Our paths had crossed a very few times since and I looked forward to a long chat. I knew he'd been working in another of the company's branches in the area and had hoped to meet up with him now I'd settled in. This was my chance to find out who was who in the area and to catch up on the gossip, what we called the grapevine.

Will carried two pints of Stowford Press cider over to join me. He looked worried.

'Have you heard about Pete Evans,' he asked as he settled down.

'Ah, my favourite bird watcher,' I took a sip of my cider. 'Ooh that's nice! I haven't seen Pete or heard anything from him since he was moved over to Norfolk. He'd been thinking of leaving the company until then, as I recall. He said he was utterly fed up last time we spoke but the offer of moving there changed his mind and he stayed with them.'

'Yes, he reckoned that was his dream job,' Will nodded. 'I remember him being so excited about the move and saying Norfolk had some of the best spots in the country for bird watching. He kept telling me that the coast of East Anglia and the Norfolk Broads are teeming with birdlife. That was more important to him than being the manager of the pharmacy I reckon. He'd probably have taken a pay cut to get that branch if they'd have asked him.'

'So what's he been up to now then?' I asked.

'Pancreatic cancer,' Will sipped his drink. 'He's very ill, the prognosis is bad.'

The pancreas is an important organ located in the upper abdomen and is composed of glands that are responsible for a wide variety of effects. For example, the exocrine glands in the pancreas secrete enzymes into the duodenum. These help in the digestion of food as it passes through the intestines. The endocrine glands secrete hormones including insulin which controls the levels of sugar in the blood.

Pancreatic cancer is not one of the most common forms of cancer but it is a rapidly growing and aggressive type. The early symptoms are usually vague, some nausea, a dull pain and some loss of appetite. Even nowadays it is a difficult cancer diagnose early enough to be able to treat it effectively. Twenty-odd years ago it was virtually impossible.

'Apparently the doctors thought he had jaundice at one stage,' Will continued. 'Then they thought he was diabetic. By the time they'd worked out it was cancer of his pancreas it was too late. There isn't much treatment available for that type of cancer anyway yet.'

*

Pete Evans died a few weeks later. Will and I had a great argument with the company over having a day or two off to go to his funeral in Norfolk. Eventually they relented and allowed us to take it as holiday. They booked a couple of relief managers and allowed us to go. That sort of thing leaves a nasty taste in your mouth.

Pete's wife, Mary, and their two children were coping marvellously well. The church was filled with his bird watching friends as well as his family, customers and neighbours. We learned that he had organised his own funeral. Pete had known his death was imminent and had made all the arrangements with the funeral director. He'd chosen the flowers he wanted, the hymns we were to sing, the music and a couple of poetry readings. Even a lunch at his favourite local overlooking a bird reserve by the marshes had been booked for us.

He hadn't wanted anyone to wear black. That would be too depressing, he'd claimed. Mary told us that initially he had demanded that everyone should wear brightly coloured frocks, high heeled shoes and large hats.

'And he said that was just for the men!' she smiled a little at the memory. 'The women could wear anything that they thought appropriate. Then he relented and said we could all please ourselves.'

After the service and burial, I stood quietly in the churchyard under the lychgate and waited as the rest of the congregation walked past me on their way down to the inn for lunch. A number of birds were chirping and singing among the bushes around the churchyard. That's the right sort of music for Pete I thought as I leaned on the ancient wooden gate to watch some jackdaws circling the church tower.

I recalled that cold dawn when Pete had dragged me from my warm bed to sit in his friend's farmyard to hear the dawn chorus, those competing robins and that blackcap. I remembered the walk we took through the woods, filled with flowers and birdsong, to warm up and stretch our legs.

That had been several years ago now but I remembered it well, and the wonderful breakfast that followed. I could still smell and taste that breakfast. I wondered how many times he had left his bed to experience that magical moment since. Many times I'd bet and knowing what Pete was like I reckoned that he'd enjoy each one as if it was the first.

Then I thought about that cricket match when Pete missed an easy catch off the TGM while bird watching. We had decided later that on the whole it had been a good thing that he had done so. The TGM would not have been pleased to be out second ball. As if we'd care about the result. It was much better that he had been allowed to score a few more runs, we reckoned.

Pete had tried to convince us that he had planned the whole thing. He didn't think any more of that type of uninspiring middle management than the rest of us but unfortunately they did have the power to promote or to leave you festering in the wilderness. Neither Pete nor I ever reached a great height in our careers but why make trouble for ourselves? We had been learning the strange ways of management slowly but surely.

I thought I was all alone by then but an elderly man, apparently the last man out of the churchyard, approached the lychgate and then paused in the shade of a nearby yew tree. He turned to look back at the new grave where some blooms glowed brightly against the flint stone wall behind. Green matting covered the pile of earth waiting to be tipped back in. It always seems strange to walk away and just leave someone like that.

'He was a lovely chap,' he said out loud to no-one in particular. 'We shall miss him.'

A robin flew down to rummage in the loose soil then went back to perch on top of the wall for a brief burst of song. He was answered by an even sharper blast of noise from a wren nearby. I recalled Pete's description of a wren's rapid song.

'I always think of wrens as having screwed-up angry faces. Think of Wayne Rooney sent tumbling in the goalmouth but denied a penalty by the referee,' he'd said.

The old man turned back and noticed me leaning on the old beam. He smiled and came up to join me, his weatherbeaten face creased in a look which suggested he didn't know me but wanted to find out who I was. It was a sort of puzzled smile, friendly as well. He shook my hand, he had a rough, strong farmer's grip.

'You're a new face, not a local chap,' he said, looking me up and down as he would have checked out a horse or bullock. 'You knew young Mr Evans I expect.'

'Oh yes,' I nodded. 'I work for the same company as he did. I didn't see him very often but we've had an adventure or two together in years past.'

'A lovely chap,' he paused and looked back at the grave again. He seemed to be lost in thought for a moment then, as if remembering something important, reached into his jacket pocket and took out his wallet. He unfolded a familiar-looking sheet of paper. An NHS prescription form.

'You'll be another chemist then?' he asked. I nodded again. 'Well look, the doc has just given me these new pills.' He handed over his prescription for me to read. 'I would've asked Mr Evans what they were for and how I must take 'em but I can't now. What d'you think?'

Well, what can you do? I went through the list of medicines and explained the use of each one then reinforced the need to comply with the doses. I mentioned the need to be sure he took one lot after meals and another one first thing in the morning with a good drink of water. Just as Pete would have done for him.

14

I think it was about that time that I decided to leave the company. The unpleasantness about getting time off for Pete's funeral had been one thing. A year or so previous to that I'd missed my sister's wedding because they cancelled the day off I'd booked months before. Then I wasn't allowed to leave work early when my dad died. I know there wasn't anything I could do but I wanted to be there with my mum. I had to wait until we closed in the evening then drive home to see her.

On another occasion when I asked for time off to go to another funeral I was told by someone in head office that the only funeral I had to attend was my own. Charming I'd thought. What an attitude! I had always tried to be flexible about booking holidays and it wasn't as if I was ever off sick.

A pharmacist who absents himself from the pharmacy without getting another one to cover for him causes a lot of trouble for the patients because the pharmacy would have had to close. He would also make a lot of trouble for himself. The company knew that and didn't bother to apologise or try to find someone to cover me and enable me to go to the wedding or that other funeral. But that's not all. It was just the last in a whole list of examples of how they treated their staff. I'd had enough of it all.

Almost twenty years before I had joined as a bright-eyed, keen young man, straight out of university and eager to work hard. At first I had considered working in a hospital pharmacy but in the 1960s there weren't many jobs for pharmacists in hospitals and the salaries offered were quite frankly insulting.

Not being bright enough to consider staying on to study to a higher level or get involved in research I had decided to go into what we then called retail pharmacy. I had the choice of working for one of the small family owned pharmacies or join one of the multiples. When I had finally qualified as a pharmacist I could have opened my own pharmacy or bought an existing one but I didn't have the experience or the funds to do so. Probably I was too scared to take the risk.

At that time the company was the only large chain of chemists although there were some small groups of co-operatives and similar concerns. Nowadays the great majority of pharmacies belong to one or other of the large chains or supermarkets and there are far fewer owner-run pharmacies in Britain.

I had thought that working for a large well-established company would be a sensible thing to do. However, over the years I found their attitude to their staff and their lack of understanding the needs of pharmacy to be both surprising and disappointing. You really think they would know better. One thing I did learn was that you get the staff you deserve. Look after them, encourage them, treat them fairly and you're at least halfway to having a successful business.

Archie's words about the company thinking that our work could be done by well-trained chimpanzees came to mind often, along with their ongoing demands to cut our banana ration by getting rid of staff, cutting their hours or replacing experienced dispensers with younger, therefore cheaper, staff.

Although bullying in the workplace was supposed to be banned many years ago it is still there. There may not be the threat of actual physical abuse nowadays but in my experience there is still a lot of what we might term mental bullying.

The 1980s brought a new young breed, some might say sub-species, of aspiring middle management. Many of the older TGMs were retired and some thrusting, as they thought of themselves, eager young district managers were sent out to stir up the rest of us.

Most of these twerps were people promoted far beyond their ability. There is a world of difference between working for a capable, supportive and knowledgeable boss and for someone who thinks he can bully people into working harder. Some people are capable of leading their staff, encouraging and thanking them. These are the good managers. Others can only push or pressurise people to work harder and harder.

Most of us would do almost anything for a good leader but the latter sort thinks it is good management to threaten staff with reduced hours or withholding pay to make them work harder. They have no intention of doing anything other than getting themselves a bigger bonus. They rarely consider a 'thank you' to be necessary.

I believe such people simply breed resentment. The staff does what they can with what resources they have but in the end they either stay to help each other cope or leave altogether rather than work harder for a company that treats its staff in this way.

By the end of the 1980s the company seemed to be hellbent on destroying the goodwill it once enjoyed from its staff and customers. There was no future there for me.

*

There are some people who enjoy the management side of the job and many who prefer the professional side of pharmacy. It takes a very determined person to do both jobs well and although it took me a while, I gradually realised that I was not such a good manager of people. I could organise myself but found it difficult to delegate to others.

This put more and more pressure on myself. There were simply not enough hours in the day to do what I wanted to do and how I wanted to do it. My performance as a pharmacist was in danger of being smothered by the role of store manager. Perhaps I was "burned out" as they say although I was barely forty years old by then. I became very disillusioned and looked around for an alternative way of making my living as a pharmacist.

All pharmacies as well as pharmacists in this country were regulated at the time by the Royal Pharmaceutical Society of Great Britain. The pharmacy premises themselves had to be registered and inspected and so were the pharmacists. One of the strictest regulations was that each pharmacy had to have a pharmacist on duty and in a position to know what was being dispensed or sold.

They had to be in a position to supervise the work going on, be able to intervene if necessary and be available to give advice and help as required. If for some reason there was no pharmacist on duty it meant having to close the pharmacy, the law was very specific about that.

The Pharmaceutical Society employed teams of pharmacy inspectors who enforced the many and varied regulations we worked with. I did think of trying to become an inspector at one period in my career. Travelling around the country inspecting other pharmacists would be preferable to being the subject of an inspection, I thought, and maybe I could do the job in a more human way. That was not to be.

Back during the 1970s and 1980s the pharmacy inspectors seemed to relish the idea of going to great lengths to trap any unwary pharmacist who dared to pop out for a quick break or even a visit to the toilet, thus leaving the pharmacy unsupervised.

There were stories of inspectors lurking in nearby shop doorways in order to observe the pharmacy and just wait for a pharmacist to leave the dispensary. They would then rush in and ask for a medicine which the assistant might sell without realising that the pharmacist wasn't in the dispensary.

The inspectors always arrived in the pharmacy unannounced in those days. Although they were invariably polite, their powers were such that one felt a surge of breathless panic at the very sight of one of them.

One of the inspectors tasks, until quite recently, was to take a sample of a dispensed prescription. They don't do that nowadays but their role is still to enforce regulations and deal with any misdemeanours. Nowadays they do at least tend to offer advice first instead of going straight for the jugular.

For the test item the inspector would take a completed prescription off the shelf from where it awaited collection by the patient. He, it was always a he in those days, would take the tablets or whatever they were out of the bottle and divide them into three piles.

One pile was taken away for analysis in a bottle which he sealed with good old fashioned red sealing wax and the other two had to be retained in case anything was wrong with the sample. The wait for the result of the test was nerve racking. We were sure it would be alright, we checked everything carefully, but everyone is human and an error could be calamitous. Even the simplest dispensing error was considered a criminal offence. We were threatened with reprimands, fines, imprisonment and being struck off the register of pharmacists for a momentary loss of concentration.

My first inspector appeared one day in Barnsgrove. I had only been working there for a few weeks and can still feel the tremor in my knees, not to mention my backbone, when he arrived. Fortunately I was in experienced hands in that pharmacy and well protected by the dispensers.

The inspector noted that I was a new student and took me aside to explain his function. This was very useful, kind of him really, some other inspectors probably wouldn't have bothered. As we talked, his back was turned to the dispensary but I could see over his shoulder that Janet, Amy and Mrs Moore were quietly removing all of the prescriptions from the ready-to-collect shelves.

They took each one out to the counter as if to hand it out to the patient but turned left and went round the back of the dispensary to put the items safely away in the stockroom. By the time the inspector had turned round to take his sample the only items on the shelf were a few bags containing specially re-checked dispensed medicines. The manoeuvre had been so carefully choreographed that he suspected nothing as took his test sample. The one they had chosen for him.

Of course, we were sure that all those other prescriptions were correct but the girls were just making sure. Human error does happen in spite of everything one tries to do and they were ensuring that the test taken from me on that day was perfect. Bless them.

*

Most pharmacies are open for six or even seven days a week. Many are open for long hours, perhaps twelve or thirteen hours a day, sometimes more. Nowadays we have pharmacies that are open for over 100 hours a week. A pharmacist has to be available all the time that the pharmacy is open. If by any chance a pharmacist is late getting to work or taken ill or absent for any reason then the pharmacy cannot operate. This is set in law for the patient's safety.

When the regular owner-pharmacist or manager is absent, for a holiday, day off or illness for example, then a locum or relief pharmacist has to be arranged. Until recent years most locum pharmacists were young newly qualified people gaining experience, older retired people doing an odd day here or there for some extra pocket money or sometimes younger women who had children and wanted to work a few flexible hours to suit their family lives.

By the end of the 1980's when I decided to go it alone, pharmacies were opening longer hours, the traditional half day had gone, more pharmacies opened on Sundays, and so more locums were required. There were just not enough retired and part-time locums to go around and it occurred to me that I might become self-employed and offer myself as a freelance locum pharmacist, working full time anywhere within about fifty miles of home.

This idea has spread among many other pharmacists especially the young newly qualified ones over the last few years. This way of working appeals to many people these days and in fact some pharmacists never become managers or are ever employed in one pharmacy. I think that I was one of the first younger or indeed middle-aged pharmacists to work independently in this way as a full time career in my part of the world and I found that this way of life suited me fine.

*

Having handed in my notice I had to say goodbye to the staff. That was the hardest bit. They had always been supportive, a grand bunch of people, and no trouble at all. Well, there was one disappointing moment just before I left when one of the stockroom staff, a man who should have known better, was caught red handed stealing tins of baby food.

At the rear of the Kemston premises was a hotel and its car park. A seven foot high brick wall separated our back yard from the parked cars belonging to the hotel's customers and staff. One of the company's security staff happened to call in to see me one day for a general chat and parked his car in a corner of the hotel's car park. While getting out of his car he was almost hit by a tin of baby food that came flying over the wall to land in a small area of weeds and grass nearby. It was followed by a second then a third.

By this time he had reached the wall and being a fit young chap had pulled himself up to be able to look over the top of the wall. Just below was a very shocked member of staff who had just fetched another couple of tins and was about to lob them over as well.

His intention was clearly to collect the tins from that quiet corner of the car park later. That member of staff left us very quickly. He was the only person I had to sack in my almost 40 years long career. It was a very nasty experience and most disappointing.

Otherwise, as I say, the staff were an excellent group and I appreciated their help many times. We all went out for a meal sometimes and I can still see the look on the faces of some young lads in the bar of a country pub on the occasion when I walked in with about twenty attractive young women. It does a man's ego a lot of good when that happens. I am pleased to be able to say that I still see many of them from time to time. In fact, I see one of them every day.

Rebecca was one of the dispensers at Kemston. She was a tall slim girl with, I thought at the time, natural blond hair. With her blue eyes and a bright cheerful attitude to life she made even the difficult days possible. She was on holiday when I started work in my new branch but when we met on her return one of the first things she told me was that Rebecca was a biblical name. In the Book of Genesis she is referred to as a maiden of beauty, modesty and kindness. Fair enough, I thought.

She could be very mischievous though. On one occasion she hid from the duty pharmacist by rolling herself up in a length of carpet. The poor man was thoroughly confused when he couldn't find her. Another time she put on a wig and glasses to play the part of someone looking for a job. That was before I arrived in the branch. The previous manager was probably relieved to be moving on.

Rebecca lived about six miles out of town and usually drove to work in a red Mini car. However, on warm summer days she would often cycle to work. Her battered old bicycle had seen better days but she invariably rode it into town whilst wearing the briefest shorts I could ever remember seeing.

I recall with a blush the evening I watched her walk away from the shop with two of her colleagues after a hectic day. I had just let them out of the front door and paused in my locking up procedure.

Rebecca was pushing the bike across the square as the three of them chatted, her long slim legs ended with pert cheeks peeping below those short shorts and once again I could hear Archie's warning words pounding through my brain.

He'd warned me about not getting too close to the staff, "I don't want any goings-on with the girls in the stockroom", he had said, and had even added, "You just watch out for those girls and stay out of trouble!".

On this occasion I ignored him and we got married a few months later.

*

Getting married and leaving a secure job for the possible vagaries of self-employment was something of a risk I know and I hit a problem almost at once. Being self-employed meant not having sick pay and one of the things I feared was ill health making it difficult for me to work. Sure I had some insurance against major illness but even just a week or two with a minor problem could make my financial situation difficult. So, taking a deep breath and hoping for the best I sent off my letter of resignation and left the comfort of a job as secure as any. The second half of my career in pharmacy began.

Unfortunately, just after I went self-employed I managed to get myself one of those dreaded hernias and had to measure myself for a truss. At least I knew how to put the thing on although I soon gained an insight to our patient's concerns and set about getting the damage repaired. Fortunately I had an excellent surgeon and after waiting a few months while wearing that truss I entered the hospital for the operation.

A hernia repair these days is fairly straightforward. A simple hernia, as opposed to a strangulated one, can be repaired under local anaesthetic and you can be in and out of hospital the same day. A couple of weeks to heal the wound and hopefully off you go, back to normal.

A couple of weeks without earning any pay was more of a worry to me at the time. I managed to just take a long weekend off resting and then work on by moving very carefully for the rest of the time. Fortunately most of my work is mental work rather than anything of a hard physical nature.

Like most people I feel nervous about having operations and anaesthetics. While I lay on the trolley waiting for the surgeon to make a start on my hernia repair I remembered the last time I'd been in hospital. I was 11 years old and had been diagnosed with appendicitis.

It was the first time I'd had to stay anywhere alone without my parents. My mother was a bit tearful when they left me at the hospital but I thought the whole thing was quite an adventure. I may not have been so lighthearted if I'd known then that my grandfather had died in that same hospital, possibly in the same operating theatre during an operation for a perforated ulcer some thirty years before.

My operation was carried out the following day and I was kept in for a few days to recover. Most of the nurses were quite nice, one of them was very pretty in fact. However there was a Scottish ward sister whose accent was so strange to me that I couldn't understand a thing she said. Also she didn't appear to move her jaw at all when speaking, whole sentences came out in one mess of letters.

A couple of days after I'd had my operation she asked me something that sounded like "yerebelsmvdtdye?" to which I said, "pardon?" After several tries and still not understanding and thinking she might be offering something unpleasant, I said a definite "No!".

Later I found out from one of the nicer nurses that she had been asking if my bowels had moved today, an expression I wouldn't have understood anyway at 11 years of age. In my innocence I had answered with a firm no! That explained the revolting stuff I was given to take which I now know to have been Senokot granules.

15

My first and most important task on becoming self employed was to make sure all the pharmacists in the area knew that I was available for locum work. I had a mortgage to pay and a new wife to support so being a freelance carried some risk. Fortunately my intuition that locum pharmacists were desperately needed proved to be correct and I soon had more than enough work to keep me occupied. I could quite easily have worked seven days a week. Rebecca was soon heard to bemoan the fact that she couldn't clone me. She would, she says, be a millionaire by now if only there were several of me.

At first I accepted every job offered. There is a feeling when you are self-employed that if you don't take on every job available then nothing will be offered in future. Having said that, there were a few pharmacies I worked in and hated. There and then I usually decided that I would not return again. I had made a start on my own little black book just as Betty had years before in Barnsgrove.

One of my first bookings was in a rather messy dispensary. The pharmacy owner's daughter was supposed to be the dispenser although I doubt she ever had any proper training. She had certainly never been shown how to do any cleaning.

Part way through the morning I went to the fridge to take out some insulin injections for a prescription. I had noticed a slight fishy smell to the place but assumed there would be a reason for that. Perhaps there was a fishmonger's shop nearby. When I opened the fridge I found the source of the smell. Two fat trout looked up at me from the shelf next to the insulin.

'There are some fish in here,' I said.

'Yes,' the owners daughter didn't look at all surprised. 'They're for my dad. One of his friends brought them in first thing this morning.'

'They'll have to go,' I said. 'You can't keep fish in the dispensary fridge.'

We had something of an argument about that but I wasn't going to put up with having fish stored with medicines. Eventually I won the argument and she reluctantly agreed to do something about them.

'I suppose I'll have to take them home then,' she muttered and added something else I pretended not to hear. She grabbed the fish in a filthy temper and stalked away. 'My dad won't like this you know!' I didn't see her again that day, nor did I ever go back to that pharmacy again. It wasn't just the episode of fish in the fridge that kept me away from that pharmacy though.

Later in the afternoon one of the local doctors came into the shop. He didn't say anything to me, in fact I hardly noticed him and didn't know he was a doctor. He selected various items from the shelves and piled them onto the counter.

'Put these on my account,' he glanced at me as I looked up but didn't speak.

The pharmacy assistant, Doreen, packed the goods for him and he left. When he had gone she came into the dispensary and took a pad from a drawer. She wrote down what the customer had taken. It was all ordinary things like shampoo, shower gel, toothpaste and a pack of antihistamine tablets.

'I suppose you send him a bill at the end of the month,' I commented although it was nothing to do with me and I wasn't really interested.

'Not really,' she said with a crafty grin. 'He doesn't pay for any of that stuff. He'll send a few prescriptions in to cover the cost more or less. I don't suppose the National Health will notice a few extra pounds to pay for his toiletries. Will they?'

The owner of the pharmacy and that doctor had obviously arranged a little scam whereby the prescriptions were written out for patients without their knowledge but were never dispensed. The taxpayer paid the pharmacy for the false prescriptions but actually paid for the doctor's family shopping.

I thought long and hard about complaining about the arrangement but I confess I didn't. Who, I wondered, would believe a story from an unknown locum pharmacist rather than an otherwise well respected doctor?

With more confidence now I would certainly make a complaint but in the event that pharmacy was sold a few months later. The old owner retired on his ill-gotten gains and his daughter got married or so I heard.

Following a few discreet enquiries I found out that the new owner had put an end to the doctor's wheeling and dealing as well. I don't suppose he was very popular with the doctor but he was braver than I had been. I just didn't ever go back to that pharmacy again. It was the first entry on my blacklist of places to avoid for my peace of mind if nothing else.

Later, when I was established, I learned to pick and choose. My place of work may have varied greatly in the state of the premises, the staff and the way they worked but I tried to make sure the job was done properly wherever I worked.

*

The main difference between starting a new career in 1968 and re-starting my career in 1989 was the change in technology. The art or science (and you can argue that one for days) of dispensing hadn't changed much in those twenty-odd years except that now we had computers.

The company I had worked for up to then had been very slow to give us computers to produce dispensing labels and for record keeping. We had been handwriting labels to stick on the bottles and jars since I started and the ordering systems still involved phoning a warehouse and reading out long lists of what was required using the phonetic alphabet. This was a very tedious business. With computer systems the ordering of stock could be done automatically as part of the dispensing process itself.

I was to find that many much smaller pharmacies, even family run ones, were way ahead of my old company. This delay in introducing new technology was mainly because my old employers had decided to develop its own computer system instead of learning from what other companies did. They missed a trick or two there and as far as I can see they still haven't caught up.

Until computers arrived in the dispensary we did not keep any record of what had been dispensed for each individual patient. The actual NHS forms had to be passed on to the Department of Health for pricing so even they disappeared from view at the end of each month. Without a complete record of what a patient was already taking it was difficult to offer safe advice on their treatment.

At that time one had to rely solely on what the patient could remember about their medication. We have never been able to access anyone's medical record as held by their doctor and it was often difficult to get any help from the doctors or their staff when a query arose. In fact there is an old pharmacist's joke. What is the difference between a doctor's receptionist and God? The answer is that God doesn't think She is a doctor's receptionist.

Private prescriptions were however recorded by copying the details by hand into a ledger and retaining the completed prescription for two years. Before the National Health Service was introduced all prescriptions were private. Many doctors invented their own products and had their own formulae in the same way that some pharmacists had their own nostrums.

Some of the doctors in the old days not only invented their favourite formulae but kept that secret by only allowing one pharmacy to make it or even by making and supplying it to their patients themselves. However, generally speaking, the details of private prescriptions had to be recorded in a prescription book.

Prescription books have been kept for many centuries. King Henry VIII had one and it is now kept and sometimes displayed in the British Library in London. His book contains several formulae, mostly of a herbal nature, which the king used. He suffered with a chronic ulcer on his leg and some of the recipes are for the "oyntments" he used. With his hectic love life he also required remedies "for the Kings grace to coole and dry and comfort the membre" but I would not dare to comment on those.

Henry VIII studied herbal healing quite seriously and some thirty of the formulae in the book are said to be of his own invention. He was apparently fascinated by the preparation and compounding of these ointments, balms, lotions and so on that he used.

He often gave advice to his court on what treatments they needed and took the necessary equipment to prepare the medicines with him on his travels. He even gave us a charter which is still the basis of the practice of herbal medicine today.

Old prescription books even from more recent times are fascinating to study if one gets the opportunity. One feels that there is always the chance of finding a long-forgotten recipe which once earned its inventor a living, and may make a bob or two for me. This hasn't yet happened yet but one of these old formulae that another pharmacist found by chance was for "Poor Man's Friend".

"Poor Man's Friend" was a widely used and popular ointment sold for headaches, bruises, gout, piles, cuts, burns and leg ulcers among other conditions. It was a so-called quack remedy invented by one Dr Giles L Roberts who opened his premises in East Street in the ancient town of Bridport in Dorset in 1788. He was unqualified at the time but later studied medicine in London and did become a licensed doctor.

Dr Roberts was a busy man. He also invented "Anti-Veneral Specific Drops" and "Alternative Pills" and his products were so popular with his customers that when he died his gravestone was engraved with the words, "His Memory is Cherished Especially by the Poor with Grateful Feelings" by his grateful clients. What more could a doctor want? The secret of his recipes were passed down through his family but then disappeared. It was assumed that the secret followed them into their graves.

"Poor Man's Friend" was made and sold for many years although many people suspected it mainly consisted of lard and sulphur. The formula was made public only recently. Some relatives of a pharmacist who had bought the doctor's old premises in Bridport during the 1970s found it among some family papers. The formula has now been placed in the Bridport museum.

The ointment was finally revealed to be 95% lard. The recipe calls for Waterford lard cut into small pieces and put in a steam apparatus with English beeswax. As the lard melted, it was drawn through cheesecloth for half an hour and the other ingredients added.

These ingredients included calomel, red precipitate, sugar of lead, something called red powder (a mixture of venetian red, best vermillion, oxide of bismuth and oxide of zinc), oil of rose, oil of bergamot and oil of lavender.

Some of these ingredients were widely used in the past, for example calomel was used as an antiseptic and to treat syphilis while zinc oxide is still used for its soothing antiseptic properties. Several of the other items would be considered too toxic to use nowadays. The ointment was sold in small pots which have themselves become quite collectable.

Although the formula is interesting from the historical point of view, unfortunately for the money-making ambitions of a pharmacist who might have found something like that, it is extremely unlikely that we would be able to supply "Poor Man's Friend" today.

Nowadays one has to prove not only that something works not just by word-of-mouth or popularity or even from an epitaph but by gathering masses of scientifically researched data. Also it would have to be shown that the drug was as safe as possible and that it wouldn't have any disastrous toxic effects. "Poor Man's Friend" would never get a product licence now.

The whole business of testing new drugs and product licencing was to see great changes after the adverse effects associated with thalidomide came to light in the early 1960s. Prior to that time many products which claimed to have a medicinal use were actually based on the "quack" remedies and "old wives tales" from the decades if not centuries before.

Few of them had been properly evaluated as to their efficacy or safety although, it has to be admitted, most of them were relatively harmless placebos. In many cases they were used simply because they always had been used and no-one thought twice about their presence in the pharmacy. As new more powerful drugs appeared in our dispensaries so the whole business of testing and developing them and the way we dispensed and sold medicines changed.

Thalidomide was widely used from 1957 to 1961. The drug was said to have been developed in Germany during the Second World War. Some people claim the Nazis discovered it during research into an antidote for nerve gas but that has proved difficult to confirm. It was found to work as an effective tranquilliser and painkiller. As there appeared to be few side effects or risk of possible overdose, thalidomide was proclaimed as a wonder drug. It was used for insomnia, headaches, colds and when it was found to be an effective anti-emetic as well, to alleviate morning sickness.

The drug testing schemes of that period were much less stringent than we use now. For example it was not thought likely that any drug could pass from the mother to her developing foetus. Thalidomide, it was said, could not cross the placental barrier. We know now of course that this theory was wrong, so terribly wrong.

The drug was withdrawn from the market in 1961 when it was realised that it was a potent teratogen. Teratogenesis is the production of a congenital bodily abnormality in a foetus. A birth defect that in this case manifested itself as a baby with abnormal limbs.

Although it was a perfectly safe drug for most patients, those pregnant mothers who were prescribed the drug were the very patients who should not have taken it at all. That is the great tragedy of thalidomide.

It was estimated that up to 20,000 children were affected worldwide and many years before any compensation was even begun to be given.

Although the drug was withdrawn in 1961 it still has some uses. It is occasionally used even today in specialist cancer clinics under strictly controlled conditions to treat cancers such as multiple myeloma and some research is being carried out into its possible use in other similar conditions.

The thalidomide tragedy led to much stricter testing being required for drugs and pesticides before they can be licensed. Many medical products that could not prove their safety either from lack of data or the fact that gathering such data would cost more than the product was worth to the manufacturer simply disappeared from the pharmacy shelves.

*

As more and more drug data became available it has become possible for pharmacists and dispensers to keep track of any potential side effects and drug interactions that might affect our patients. The use of computer systems to record what each patient had been given along with this growing knowledge is probably one of the greatest changes in recent years as far as the safer administration of medicines is concerned.

A patient who has all of his or her prescriptions dispensed in their regular pharmacy will build up a record of medication. We still don't have access to patient's medical records held by their doctors or any knowledge of the results of any tests they may have had taken or information from hospital treatments.

However, if for example a doctor adds a new drug into the patient's regime the pharmacist will be able to compare that new drug with his current medication record and highlight any probable interaction between the two. This was simply not possible in most instances before patient medication records began to be kept on the dispensary computer. Here is an example.

A young woman who has been taking the oral contraceptive tablet is prescribed a course of antibiotics for some reason or another. Perhaps she has seen her dentist or had to visit a hospital or a nurse at work. We know that some antibiotics can interact with the contraceptive pill which may cause the contraception to fail resulting in an unwanted pregnancy, then perhaps leading to the patient having an abortion.

If the young lady brings her prescription to her usual pharmacy the dispenser will enter the details into the patient record. The system will automatically compare this new drug, the antibiotic, with what she is already taking, the contraceptive. The interaction will be highlighted and in that case the pharmacist would have to refer back to the prescriber.

Thus the patient will not risk a pregnancy she doesn't want, possibly can't afford, and will hopefully be pleased with his intervention. Often in my experience she will complain like hell for being kept waiting while the pharmacist sorts out an alternative with the prescriber but we just have to accept that, I suppose.

*

As it happens that example of an interaction between a contraceptive and an antibiotic was almost the first prescription I was to see when I became a self-employed locum pharmacist. I found the different computer systems a little bewildering at first but also found that despite their differences they all did the same job in the end.

Recording the dispensing of any prescription in the computer always begins with the patient's name and address. I have been amused over the years by the changes in fashion for names. Older patients for example were usually called Margot or Hilda or Edna or Harold or George or William. Many old names have come back into fashion, we see lots of Georges and Henrys nowadays although I can't remember a young Edna recently.

I sometimes pity the poor children who are named after the latest pop singer, actor, holiday destination or food. They must spend all their lives explaining who or what they were named after or indeed how to spell it. Picture the girl who has to introduce herself as Teekeelya and explain that her mother had probably drunk far too much of the stuff before choosing the name.

Some names have more of an attraction after one hears the story. A prescription came in for a baby called Ypres. I knew about the First World War and its terrible battles and thought it was an interesting idea for a name as I typed it into the computer. The mother seemed to feel some explanation was required and told me her story. I wonder how many times she and the child will have to repeat it in future. It was quite a straightforward tale.

Just before the baby was born the mother had been researching her family history. She found out that her great-great-grandfather had died at Ypres and wanted to record the fact. She would take her daughter to visit the battlefield and the cemetery where he was laid when she was old enough to understand.

I have seen prescriptions for a child named Nuggett and another called Garland and I didn't really want to know why but their parents also felt the need to explain. Nuggett because "she's pure gold". Actually I thought a gold nugget was the way gold was found naturally and not pure gold at all but contained various impurities. I didn't bother to say so. I was just happy for the child that she wasn't named after a chicken nugget.

Garland was, as you guessed, born on Christmas Eve. Then there was a Uganda who turned out to be a cute little blue-eyed blond girl and a Lululu who's mother clearly didn't know when to stop.

*

One of my early locum jobs involved a long drive through the floods caused by a summer storm to the lovely riverside town of Evesbridge. I was almost late arriving as I had to try three different roads to get across the river Severn. The first one I tried was blocked by a red Fiat Panda. I rounded a corner to find the car bobbing along the flooded road towards me. There was no-one inside so I assumed it had been abandoned earlier.

Driving carefully down the next road I made sure the floods were not too deep by judging that I was safe where I could see the grass verge above the muddy water and make out the white line in the middle of the road even though it was submerged. Then I met a man in a large lorry.

The driver signalled to me to stop as he approached. I wound down my window and looked up. He leaned out of his cab and pointed to a sort of high water mark on the side of the door.

'Just back down the road the water came up to there mate,' he grinned. 'You'll have to go back.'

The line was about level with my ear as I sat in my seat. I turned round and went back to find another route.

I managed to get to the pharmacy at last but was surprised to find myself standing outside a small church. The church had been a hospital chapel for many years before being deconsecrated and converted into a pharmacy. It made for a very strange almost surreal sight as I pushed open a huge wooden door studded with nails and entered.

Inside, from the ground level up to about seven feet high it was a normal pharmacy. The usual shelves and fittings held medicines, cosmetics, health foods, toiletries of many and varied kinds and baby merchandise. Looking up above the canopy over the shelf fittings however and it was still a church.

The roof beams and trusses, the tall narrow stained glass windows, marble memorials and the religious statuary were all there. The shop floor had been laid out where the nave had once been with the counter stretching from side to side across the step up to the chancel. The dispensary filled the space left behind when the choir and alter had been removed.

The whole dispensary was lit by stained glass windows depicting God, Jesus, various saints, angels and cherubs around and above. It was a very peculiar feeling to stand at the workbench dispensing a prescription with St Matthew and St Mark looking over one shoulder, St Luke and St John peering over the other and a round window filled with an image of God greeting Jesus in heaven right behind me. I felt that they might have been making another check on my accuracy. Still, every little bit of help is acceptable I suppose.

A mother with a lad of about 10 years of age was waiting for his medication when I arrived. He had another unforgettable name. His parents had chosen two hyphenated christian names for him intending no doubt to give him the best start in life. Many times over the years I have wondered what became of him when he grew up. He would be, I feel, in a good position to succeed.

Lucky-Boy Lewis, champion jockey perhaps, or a successful race horse trainer. Perhaps he'd build up a large chain of betting shops or run a bingo hall. Maybe he'd be a world champion boxer, there was something of the fairground boxing booth about his look, or a successful politician. I haven't noticed him in the papers yet so maybe his luck ran out but I did wish him well.

It still surprises me that here in the twenty-first century there are quite a few people who have never learned to read and write. This becomes apparent in the pharmacy when the patient or their representative has to fill in the reverse of the prescription form.

In passing, may I inform the world that the need to fill in the back of your prescription is not something that we in the pharmacy have dreamt up to make your life difficult. In truth it makes our lives more difficult and being abused while you are trying to do your job is not pleasant.

The back of the NHS prescription form is filled in when the patient wishes to claim that they are exempt from paying the prescription charge. This charge or levy is not paid to the pharmacist or his staff. It is not a dispensing fee or a contribution to the cost of running the pharmacy. The prescription charge is a tax. Let us get that straight. It is a tax. Like every other tax, be it road vehicle tax, income tax, insurance tax, airport tax, fuel tax, valued added tax and so on it is collected by someone like us and has to be passed on to the Treasury.

The Chancellor of the Exchequer and his minions then decides what to do with it. The money may be used to pay for all sorts of things. It may be put towards building schools, for example or to pay for the health service, to buy bombs and nuclear submarines or even build up a generous pension pot for politicians and civil servants. Bitter? Me?

Patients often think we should sign the back of the forms for them. It is a nuisance I'm sure to have to get your glasses out and pick up a pen. The problem is that we don't always know for sure that the patient is exempt from paying the charges, or indeed why, so if we sign for them we become liable for any illegal claim they might make. I don't see why we should have to take that risk. Also we have enough to do without doing something that you, the patient, could easily do yourselves.

In recent years the Department of Health has made an enormous effort to catch people who cheat the prescription tax system and we would be the ones in trouble if we make a false claim on your behalf. Do please sign your own prescriptions in future. In fact if all patients filled them in before coming to the pharmacy it would speed up the dispensing process no end. Sometimes, however, it is interesting to watch a patient as they fill in the back of the prescription form...

I was working in a pharmacy in Belmont Bridge one day when a middle-aged couple approached the dispensary with a prescription to be dispensed. The man carefully placed the form down on the counter but hesitated as he reached out to pick up a pen. He leaned forward to study the form for a moment then straightened up and put the pen down again. He said something I didn't quite catch to his wife.

She helped him off with his jacket and cardigan. As she folded them neatly and put them on a chair, he began to roll up the shirt sleeve covering his left arm. When he was ready he leaned his left elbow on the counter with his forearm flat in front of him and put the prescription form just in front of his arm. Then he picked up the pen again and began to write. His face was screwed up in concentration and a few beads of sweat appeared on his brow as he copied the name tattooed on his forearm onto the back of the form.

I realised that he couldn't write his own name but at some time in his life he had learned to copy it. Perhaps a teacher or parent or someone had written his name down for him to copy in an attempt to try and teach him to write. Clearly he knew what his name looked like.

I imagine he must have had a moment of inspiration at some stage and had his name tattooed there on his forearm where he could see it and copy it whenever he had to sign anything. He had overcome his lack of education in a rather clever way and I felt a moment of admiration for him.

16

The car park at the foot of Corndon Hill was almost full by the time we arrived. It was still only about seven o'clock on a bright June morning when our minibus slotted into a spare corner and a rather nervous-looking group of us climbed out. As I swung my rucksack up onto my shoulder I collided with a man wearing a red anorak, tweed plus fours and a well-worn pair of walking boots.

'Oops! Sorry!' I offered as he winced. He glared at me, his stare was quite unnerving, and then he just grunted as he walked away.

'Well, that's a good start,' I said to those nearest to me as the rest of the passengers got out and assembled to await instructions.

I looked around the crowd milling in the car park and noted that many of them were much better prepared for this walk than I was. Everyone else looked fit and healthy, almost without exception kitted out in boots and backpacks. Even, I noticed, a few bobble hats. There were cheerful smiles and brown knees as far as the eye could see. These people mean business, I thought with a glance at my own more casual outfit. But then until a few days ago I hadn't really intended to be there at all.

I had been booked in to work for only one day as a locum pharmacist in a pharmacy near Shrewsbury. I had not worked at that one before but I had enjoyed the day. It was a busy place with quite a lot of dispensing to do and an interesting assortment of questions to deal with but it hadn't been unreasonably demanding. They had a well laid out dispensary and sufficient staff. We managed to clear all the work and still had the occasional moment for a chat. Those are my favourite sort of days.

The pharmacy was modern and well run and its staff were a pleasant crew of mainly middle-aged women. There had been some talk of a charity walk during the day and then during the afternoon one of them, Alice, explained some of the details. She began by telling me that it was called The Six Summits Walk because the route took them up and down six of Shropshire's hills.

'We start on Corndon Hill,' Alice was, I gathered, the keenest walker and had actually completed the whole walk the previous year. 'Then across to the top of the Stiperstones where you have to touch the Devil's Chair before dropping down to cross a small stream, the East Onny. Then you go up over the Long Mynd and down into Church Stretton.

We have a break for lunch there then we go up and over Caer Caradoc. It is all country lanes after that until you get over Wenlock Edge and up to Abdon Burf on Brown Clee hill. Then more road walking until you reach the last climb up to Titterstone Clee. We will finish in the quarry just below the radar dish on top of the hill.'

'That sounds like an awful lot of up,' I commented, feeling breathless just listening to her.

'The top of Corndon Hill, the first one, is at 513 metres,' she replied. 'The last summit at Titterstone Clee is 523 metres so we only go up ten metres altogether.' I gave her my best disbelieving look. She continued. 'The other hills are all about the same height, its the ups and downs between them that make your legs ache.' She laughed. 'And the miles of walking in between of course.'

The walk had been organised to raise money for various charities and involved walking up to 36 miles over the beautiful south Shropshire hills. My colleagues explained that one didn't have to walk the whole distance as there were several checkpoints from which the organisers would ferry those who wanted to stop back to their vehicles. There was a time limit as well so only the very keen and committed walkers were likely to complete the whole route. It all sounded very well planned and, as I remarked, I'm sure it would be a lovely thing to do on a nice day.

The girls filled in a few more details as we worked and, although I didn't realise it for a while, they were gradually beginning to include me in their plans. Reflecting on the day later when I got home, I thought how neatly they had ensured my participation. No-one actually asked if I would go along with them. One minute *they* were going to do this walk and the next, it seemed, *we* were going to do it.

As we sorted ourselves out in the car park a woman with a very worried look on her face approached us. She said she was looking for her husband.

'He's about my height,' she said. 'In his sixties. He's wearing a red anorak and plus fours. He will wander off if I don't watch him. Have any of you seen him please?'

'I saw someone like that a couple of minutes ago,' I said. 'I'm afraid I bumped into him. He went round the front of the bus, I think, that way.' She hurried away and a little while later I noticed the two of them waiting hand-in-hand near the start of the walk and thought nothing more about them.

We lined up for a group photo, the girls from the pharmacy and me. I did wonder at the time whether it was because they didn't expect us all to be together at the end of the walk for a triumphant pose or if they would use the photos when they came looking for anyone who disappeared by the wayside. By the time everyone had the photos they wanted most of the walkers were well up the first hill. We joined the remaining queue for the start.

That first hill almost finished me off. The path left a checkpoint in the car park, climbed up a near vertical bank, over a wire fence then straight up to the top of the hill. The fitter walkers overtook me as I coughed and spluttered my way up. At the top I sat down to get my breath back and another man collapsed beside me. He pointed to another hill a short way off to the west.

'That hill is called Lan Fawr,' he puffed. 'That's Welsh for Big Hill. I suppose we should be thankful that we're going the other way.'

A loose line of walkers filed across the fields and through the woods ahead of me. Small groups collected together, chatted among themselves, then separated as the pace varied between them. We solitary souls plodded on.

The temperature was rising by the time I reached the Devil's Chair and if it had looked more comfortable I might well have settled into it for the rest of the day. I had drunk most of the water I'd set out with but fortunately the stewards at the checkpoints had a plentiful supply for us.

The rocks that make up the Devil's Chair are of a unique material called Stiperstones Quartzite. Alice had told me that they were supposed to have been carried there by the Devil himself.

For some reason he was taking them in his apron to fill in a neighbouring valley. Unfortunately for him the strings of his apron broke and scattered the rocks on the crest of the Stiperstones hill. He left them there in disgust and it is said that in hot weather you can still smell the brimstone on them. I did bend down to take a sniff, risking a burned nose, but they just smelled like hot rocks in the sun to me.

According to the local legend the Devil sits on his chair on the longest night of the year. All his local followers, witches and the like, are summoned to meet there to choose their king for the year.

By the time I'd reached Caer Caradoc I'd had enough. The countryside was beautiful, the hills and fields spreading out giving glorious views in all directions but I know my limits. I do love walking but I rarely walk more than twelve or fifteen miles and by that point my knees were hurting and my feet sore.

I had done four out of the six summits and by the time I reached the next checkpoint would have completed two-thirds of the distance. However I am a slow walker, I amble rather than stride out, so I was bound to run out of time to complete the walk.

Many of the other walkers had passed me by as we walked but I had enjoyed a few companionable conversations with a wide variety of people. Having raised a little money in sponsorship, I felt I'd done my bit for the cause. It had all made for a very enjoyable day.

Near the summit of Caer Caradoc I stopped for a rest and sat down next to the couple I'd spoken to in the car park before we started. They had been ahead of me all the way by varying distances but I had noticed their steady progress as they walked, always hand-in-hand. I had the impression that the woman was leading the man, encouraging him as they went, sometimes stopping to point out a particular place in the wonderful view and all the time holding tightly to his hand.

'You found him alright then,' I said as I sat down. She looked puzzled. 'You were looking for your husband in the car park. I'm the one who bumped into him when I got off the bus.' She nodded.

'Yes, I like to keep an eye on him. He tends to wander off when I'm not looking,' she hesitated. 'He gets a bit confused sometimes.'

We talked a little about the walk and what a beautiful area of countryside it covered. She told me that she and her husband had done the same walk a few years before with some friends. It had rained the whole way but they'd had a fantastic time.

On this occasion she had been trying to remind him of the earlier walk by talking about those old friends and pointing out particularly lovely views but, she told me sadly, he couldn't remember much.

'I don't suppose we'll be doing this sort of thing together for much longer,' she said with a faint smile.

I told her how I'd become involved in the walk in the first place. The rest of the staff from the pharmacy had either gone on ahead or given up by that time so I could lay the blame firmly at their feet, sore or otherwise. I assumed Alice had already finished the route.

'So you're a pharmacist?' she asked. I confessed. 'You will know about Alzheimer's disease then.'

Alzheimer's disease is a common brain disorder which features the loss of nerve tissue such as neurons and synapses and shows up in the appearance of tangled masses of microscopic fibres in the brain cells. The disease has a progressive pattern of cognitive and functional impairment. In the early stages the only symptoms may be forgetfulness and an inability to plan ahead or remain attentive.

Like this man, the patient may become restless, he was wandering around the car park even though his wife had asked him to wait in their car while she checked them in for the walk. I had noticed the wild stare and confused look when I collided with him.

'The doctors are still doing tests,' She added in a quiet voice. 'They say they can't give him any drugs to help yet. Maybe when he's worse they might do something.' She squeezed his hand and kissed his cheek.

There are four medicines available in this country to help manage Alzheimer's disease. We know that a neurotransmitter called acetylcholine carries nerve impulses across synapses or junctions in the brain. In Alzheimer's this activity is known to be reduced so three of these four drugs work by trying to increase the amount of acetylcholine available. They reduce the rate at which the transmitter is broken down by inhibiting an enzyme called acetylcholinesterase. Donepezil (branded as Aricept), galantamine (Reminyl) and rivastigmine (Exelon) are the three drugs available.

The fourth drug, memantine (or Ebixa), acts on a different neurotransmitter called glutamate. Any of these medicines may be used at various stages of Alzheimer's disease but none of them will halt the progression of the disease.

'There is a lot of research going on.' This was the only encouragement I could offer. 'One day we might have a cure, I do hope so. In the meantime there is the Alzheimer's Society. They offer a lot of advice and support. If you haven't got their address I'm sure your local pharmacist will have it.'

We walked down Caer Caradoc together. The woman spoke of her fears for the future, of how she would have to care for him as his disease progressed. She knew it would bring more and more pressure on her and dreaded the thought of having to put him in a home if she couldn't cope. It was such a glorious day for a walk in the country but that was over-shadowed by the thought that these two lovely people might not get to share many more like it together in the future.

*

I was still thinking about the couple I met on that charity walk as I drove to work in a pharmacy in Tewkesbury a few days later. It was another beautiful June morning and I crossed the Malvern Hills whilst listening to a tape of Edward Elgar's music.

My pleasure in the music and the lovely day contrasted in my mind with the sad future of the woman who would have to spend her next few years looking after the man she loved. If she were here would she, I wondered, see the same beauty in the morning, could she hear, in her imagination perhaps, the same soundtrack to compliment the view or would she be sadly contemplating a grim future as a carer.

The small market town of Tewkesbury lies where two of England's loveliest rivers, the Severn and the Warwickshire Avon join. I like the place a lot, it has an immense amount of history. The Romans and the Saxons were both here and then the Normans arrived and among other things founded the magnificent Tewkesbury Abbey. Some experts tell us that the beautiful stone used by Robert FitzHamon to build it came by sea and river from his homeland at Caen in Normandy. Others say the stone might have been brought from Bredon Hill or the Cotswolds and even then it would have come by river, in that case along the Avon.

The town still has many old timber-framed and brick buildings some of which date as far back as the 15th century. There are dozens of narrow alleyways burrowing between them. I arrived in plenty of time and explored some of the maze of tiny alleys and lanes overlooked by the wonderful abbey, eventually finding my way to the pharmacy I was looking for.

I have often been struck by how similar many of our pharmacies are. The premises come in all shapes and sizes of course but the layout inside is fairly standard. There is a counter, usually offering over-the-counter medicines and a space for patients to fill in the back of their prescriptions. Shelves of vitamins, herbal medicines, baby products and toiletries surround the walls and often you will find perfumes and cosmetics as well. A photographic section or even a pet medicines display may be there.

I have also noticed a distinctive smell to pharmacies. It is a mixture of baby powder and other perfumes sometimes mixed with polish or whatever they washed the floor with.

In the dispensary the computer systems may vary along with the different owners but mostly I have found the work is very much the same wherever I may be. The staff vary a lot in their knowledge and attitude but they are invariably friendly and helpful. Those in Tewkesbury got off to a splendid start by having a cup of tea ready for me even as I walked in through the door. This is my sort of pharmacy.

Around mid-morning, a lady of about 65 years of age came in and asked to see the pharmacist. She told the pharmacy assistant that she had a query about travel medicines. She explained that after looking after her ailing parents for many years she was now free to travel. Both of them had now died and she had no other family having given up her career and a possible family of her own to stay at home with them.

'Where are you thinking of going,' I asked.

'South America, all being well, and I'd really love to go to the Galapagos and to Easter Island,' she replied and the excitement sparkled in her eyes. 'I'm going to have my gap year now,' she went on with a giggle. 'I didn't get chance before. In fact I don't think they'd been invented when I left school.'

'Good for you,' I said. 'I'm very envious.'

'I've been discussing my route with a travel agent and she said I would probably need to get some malaria tablets for parts of the journey. I might have to go and see my doctor I suppose but its always awkward to get an appointment just to ask him anything so I thought I'd see what you think.'

'Right. Well it depends where you go in South America,' I said reaching for my chart of recommended antimalarial drugs. 'I know you won't need them for Easter island or the southern parts of Chile or Argentina but you will need them for some other areas. Where exactly are you going?'

'I want to start in Buenos Aires then travel down through Patagonia to Tierra del Fuego. Then up through southern Chile to Santiago. I can fly from there to Easter Island and then when I get back I want to go north across the Atacama desert to Bolivia. I want to visit Lake Titicaca. From there I am going to La Plaz then into Peru for Cuzco and Machu Picchu.' She paused to gather her thoughts.

'Well you are certainly making up for lost time,' I was astonished by her plan. 'It will take a whole gap year if not more to do that journey.'

'There's more,' she grinned. 'I thought of going further up through Colombia but it looks terribly dangerous. All those drug gangs and so on. So I am travelling down the Amazon river instead. I had thought of going to the Galapagos as well but I haven't quite worked out how to fit that in yet. I have to go through Ecuador it seems. What tablets will I need if I do that as well?'

'Prophylaxis for malaria has to take into account the risk of exposure to malaria and the extent of drug resistance as well as any possible side effects,' I replied as I checked the chart. 'Also it will depend on what are called patient related factors such as your age, other health problems and medication. You'll probably need to have some travel injections as well. You will have to see the doctor or nurse for those in plenty of time before you leave.'

'I'm not taking any other medication,' she replied. 'The last time I saw my doctor he said I was as fit as a flea.'

'Good good. Some parts of your route carry what is known as a variable to high risk of malaria. Some parts of Peru, Bolivia and Ecuador would fall into that category. You should take prophylaxis if you are visiting those particular zones. The Amazon basin would present the highest risk and for that section of your journey you would definitely need to take some antimalarial prophylaxis.'

'Can I buy what I need or do I have to get a prescription?'

'The recommended prophylaxis is either mefloquine 250mg weekly, doxycycline 100mg daily or Malarone daily. All of them are prescription only medicines I'm afraid so you'll have to see your doctor. He'll have to discuss with you which one will be most appropriate for you individually.

You will need to tell him how long you will be in the risk areas because you have to start some tablets before you enter the risk area and continue for some weeks after you leave. Your prescription will need to be for sufficient tablets to cover your travels.

'Also I'm afraid the National Health Service will not pay for malaria prophylaxis so you'll get a private prescription and have to pay the cost of the medication.'

'Oh well,' she smiled again. 'It's worth it I suppose. I don't want to come back with malaria, do I? The trip will cost a lot of money anyway so I don't suppose the cost of the medicines will make a huge difference to the total.'

'That's the best answer I've ever heard to that problem,' I had expected her to complain about having to pay for the necessary drugs. Most people do even though, as she said, the cost of the drugs is only a fraction of the cost of the holiday or indeed the potential problems of catching malaria.

'Well, I hope you have a lovely trip,' I added. 'Don't forget me if you want someone to come along to carry your suitcase.'

17

What would you think if you picked up a bottle of tablets in your local pharmacy and read the name N-(4-hydroxyphenyl) acetamide on the label? Or possibly one labelled as C8H9NO2? I suspect the vast majority of people would be thoroughly confused. Then perhaps on another occasion you might have to ask for a pack of 2-(4-Iso Butyl Phenyl) Propionic Acid or even C13H18O2.

Chemical nomenclature is a very precise means by which everyone involved in researching, manufacturing or developing medicines can be sure that they know exactly what another person anywhere in the world is referring to in any language.

Mercifully for the rest of us and in particular for the patient in the pharmacy, medicines are usually given much simpler names. In this case the first one will be better known to most people as paracetamol, a well known painkiller, and the second example is ibuprofen which is used for its anti-inflammatory effect.

Paracetamol and ibuprofen are also available under many brand names both alone and in combination with other medicines. This system of marketing whereby one active ingredient can be found in many different forms and disguised by several brand names can lead to some problems.

There are literally hundreds of brands of painkillers to be found on a pharmacy's counter and shelves. Each manufacturer tries to ensure that their product is the one bought by advertising and recommending its use as an analgesic or for cold and 'flu or period pain and so on. What no-one tells you is that all of them contain one or other of just three active ingredients. Whatever the brand name or manufacturer or celebrity recommendation for an over-the-counter painkiller you pick up they are all either aspirin, paracetamol or ibuprofen or a combination of them.

Paracetamol in its correct dose is a perfectly safe form of medication. Millions of doses of paracetamol are taken every day without problem. It is however very easy to take too high a dose in error. I have come across customers wanting to buy an own brand paracetamol tablet, a pack of Panadol (which is also paracetamol) and one of Lemsip (also containing a normal dose of paracetamol) and all at the same time.

If that patient had a bad cold and headache she might be tempted to take a dose of each preparation. This could easily lead her to an overdose of paracetamol, perhaps to her death. Those of us involved in selling medicines have to be aware of the possibilities of these tragedies and have a responsibility to ask questions to ensure the purchase is appropriate.

Some patients also seem to believe that if taking two paracetamol tablets works alright then taking four or six of them will work twice or, better still, three times as well. Again this could lead to an overdose. People have died when trying to put such ideas to the test.

*

Miss Watkins was for many years a regular customer in the Ludford pharmacy. The staff knew her well and when I was the locum pharmacist there one day I met her too.

'Is my prescription ready?' she snapped across the dispensary counter.

'What name and address is that please?' I asked.

'They know me here,' her frosty glare and thin lipped pout suggested she found the question to be an unnecessary and irrelevant irritation. One of the dispensers who knew her all too well fetched the completed prescription for me. I began to check, as I always do, that she knew which medicines were there, and what to do with them.

'I know about the medicines, I am a nurse you know,' she snatched up the bag, tore off the prescription form and tossed it down onto the counter in front of me.

I watched her turn to put the bag into her shopping trolly, saving my breath and thinking all the while about that old pharmacist's joke; what is the difference between a retired nurse and God? The answer is that God doesn't think she's ... but you already know the answer to that one.

Nurses, by and large, do a fantastic job and I have met and worked with several who specialise as, for example, theatre nurses or in midwifery. I have also worked alongside many community nurses who give an excellent service.

They, like pharmacists, have found themselves taking on much of the workload previously done by the over-pressed doctors. The government has discovered that in many instances we can do just as good a job as the doctors used to do, and we are a lot cheaper too.

However if there is an equivalent of a red rag to a bull in the pharmacy it is the nurse who says, "I am a nurse!" as if that means she knows more about the medicine than the pharmacist. Often the culprit is someone who was trained many many years ago. Miss Watkins was a prime example of the type.

She was, according to her prescription, 72 years old. Clearly her training had probably taken place fifty years ago. She may well have worked in nursing for many years of course and would have been in her time, I'm sure, a perfectly capable one.

Those who trained her would probably have worked through the Second World War. They would have seen some terrible sights and I wouldn't want to have been there myself. Those are the nurses who have all my admiration. I know they would have trained our Miss Watkins very well. She would know all about the techniques used at that time. In the 1950s, that is.

I may be accused of a generalisation here but in my experience retired nurses like Miss Watkins tend to conform to a particular pattern. They can often be recognised by their appearance alone but as soon as that first barked order is uttered, you just know. They don't ask you to do something, they order you around.

They are also among the most impatient of a population who expects their prescription to be done immediately, "it's only a few pills so what's taking you so long?" is the standard nonsense one hears. They really believe that their prescription is of course the only one in the dispensary at the time and refuse to believe there could possibly be a query which needs to be sorted out first.

Elderly retired nurses of the Miss Watkins type tend to have short tidy hairstyles. They were ordered by matron to look like that in 1950 and have never changed. A few admittedly may have dared to grow their hair into a short bob and a very few have allowed curls to appear but not many. Gee-gaws and fripperies are not tolerated.

They do not wear much makeup, perhaps a meagre smear of lipstick, and only display one ring or a pair of tiny earrings but little other jewellery. Again that's the way they were taught. Sensible shoes will be worn naturally and her coat or jacket will always carry the defining symbol of a retired nurse - one of those small upside down fob watches on a chain pinned to the lapel.

Miss Watkins finished zipping up her trolley and turned to leave. She checked the time on her tiny dangling watch and took a couple of paces away from the dispensary. She stopped and took out her purse then used one hooked finger to claw the pharmacy assistant towards her.

'I want some ibuprofen tablets,' she straightened her finger to point at the shelf behind the girl. 'Two hundred micrograms will do.'

'They're two hundred milligrams actually,' the pharmacy assistant said, correcting her in a friendly tone and then, noticing the glare, probably wishing she hadn't bothered.

Knowing that Miss Watkins had just collected a prescription the girl turned to ask me if selling the ibuprofen to her would be alright. I picked the form up off the counter and also checked the computer record to see what medication she was supposed to be taking.

'Well no.' I said to Miss Watkins. 'You are already taking a medicine called Arthrotec which contains diclofenac. Diclofenac is a non-steroidal anti-inflammatory drug so you wouldn't want to take another one of the same type like ibuprofen at the same time.

'Also the Arthrotec contains an ingredient intended to protect your gastro-intestinal system from any ulceration which could be caused by the diclofenac. Again taking ibuprofen might make any side effects even worse. I would not advise that you buy ibuprofen.'

Again the frosty, tight-lipped stare. Someone, me, this awkward stranger, not much more than half her age, had dared to question her knowledge. I tensed myself for an argument. I really was not going to allow my colleague to sell ibuprofen to her in these circumstances. It would be irresponsible of me to do so. Telling Miss Watkins that my advice was for her own good would be a waste of time of course.

There was a moment of silence, the pharmacy staff held their breath. Miss Watkins turned away and dragged her shopping trolley out of the pharmacy. Everyone breathed again.

It is quite possible that she would go and buy her ibuprofen from another pharmacy or indeed another shop. You can buy them from all sorts of places including garages and corner shops where no-one would be able to advise her. I hope her training as a nurse included a lesson or two in common sense and that, on reflection, she would see the sense in what she had been told. Not that she would admit that to a mere pharmacist of course.

*

About six weeks later I was booked to work for another day in that same pharmacy in Ludford. During the course of the day I met another local nurse. This time it was a much more pleasant experience.

The pharmacy was one of the few independently owned pharmacies left in the town. In fact it was one of the few left in the county. Nearly all the others within about forty miles of my home have become branches of one or other of the larger chains, groups or supermarkets.

Shirley, the owner of the business as well as the pharmacist, had fought off all attempts to get her to sell out to the big companies. She was passionate about her work, had a lovely staff including two very experienced dispensing technicians and took pains to be involved in any local initiatives where she felt she could help. One such initiative was the training of nurses to prescribe certain treatments.

This was one of the Department of Health's more sensible decisions and set out to remove some of the unnecessary work previously carried out by doctors. One suspects that the Department had considered the cost savings rather than any convenience to the patient but in the event it has proved to be a good idea.

Up until recently only practitioners like doctors and dentists could write NHS prescriptions. This meant that, for example, each time a nurse wanted some dressings for one of her patients she had to order a prescription from the receptionist and when available the prescription then had to be signed by a doctor. This could take some time in busy surgeries and might delay a visit by the nurse to change a patient's dressings.

It made perfect sense to allow suitably qualified nurses to write their own prescriptions for a range of products which could then be dispensed and supplied to the patient with a minimum of delay. Shirley had become involved in the training that the nurses received to prepare them for the day when they could legally write prescriptions.

'Oh hello, is Shirley about?' a voice from across the counter distracted me as I was checking a prescription.

'No, sorry, she's away today. I'm Paul Rodgers, a locum pharmacist. Can I help?' I had looked up to find one of the community nurses had arrived. She looked worried and came into the dispensary clutching a pad of blank prescription forms and a copy of the Drug Tariff with a pen stuck in it, apparently to mark a particular page.

'I'm sorry to bother you,' she said. 'My name's Sue. I've got to write a prescription for one of my patients. She needs some dressings and surgical tape. I'm on my way to visit her this afternoon.'

'That's OK,' I gave her my friendly, encouraging smile.

'It will be the first time I've ever written a prescription,' she pulled a scary face then smiled. 'Would you mind watching me and telling me if I write everything down properly. Shirley did my training and she said I could come in if I wasn't sure about anything.'

'Fire away.'

Sue opened her Drug Tariff which lists all the dressings and appliances she was allowed to prescribe. She had already written the patient's details on the form and proceeded to copy the description of the dressings she wanted from the book. She added the size she required and a quantity of ten dressings and then ordered one roll of surgical tape giving its dimensions as well. Then she tore off the form with a theatrical flourish and handed it to me.

'That's perfect,' I said. 'If you always copy the full description from the book like that we'll have no problems at all in dispensing what you order. I'm glad you entered a proper quantity as well. That really is an excellent prescription.'

'Shirley warned us about the quantities,' she grinned. 'I gather there have been lots of problems in the past. She told us to always write a proper figure then we all know where we are.'

The nurse watched as I entered the details into the computer system and produced the necessary labels. One of the dispensers had already fetched the dressings and tape from the stockroom and within minutes we had completed the whole job.

'Easy,' Sue said.

'Easy when we have all the details.' I replied and filed the prescription away with the other completed forms.

'What happens to that form now?' she asked as I put the items into a bag for her.

'We have to sort the forms in a particular order, count them and file them in bundles. We have to do that before they can be sent to the National Health Service's pricing division at the end of the month. There they total up the costs and pay for the medicines and dressings or whatever. The prescription form basically becomes an invoice to charge the cost to the taxpayer.'

'Would I be able to get the form back later?' She hesitated while looking faintly embarrassed. 'It sounds stupid I expect but I wondered if I could keep the form and frame it. It is my first one ever!'

'We won't see it again, so sorry but no,' I thought for a second. 'We could photocopy it if you like and you could take that and frame it as a souvenir.'

So we did. Strictly speaking we are not supposed to photocopy prescription forms but I reckoned this was for Sue's own personal record. She was proud to be a prescribing nurse now, so why not?

*

The ability of prescribers other than doctors and dentists to issue prescriptions was one of the big changes to the way patients obtain their medicines in recent years. As well as appropriately trained nurses, some pharmacists can also write prescriptions for certain medicines now. There are even greater changes on the way.

The paper prescription forms that have served us for so long are set to disappear at some time in the future. We have been hearing about electronic prescriptions for years now but the idea is at last slowly gathering momentum.

The Electronic Prescription Service, known as EPS, is being developed and implemented by the Department of Health, pharmacies and computer software developers so that patient's prescriptions can be sent electronically between the GP's surgery, the pharmacy and the prescription pricing division.

At present over 1.3 million paper prescriptions are issued each working day and this figure is rising by around 5% a year. This paper-based system is overloaded and the intention is to do away with paper almost completely by the introduction of the new computer systems and software which are now being tested and installed.

A number of pilot projects have been run to test various ways of transmitting the prescriptions and to enable computer software developers to come up with suitable equipment which will work out in the real world.

The current system requires a paper form to be written by the doctor or other prescriber or printed off by the surgery staff and signed by the doctor. This is the same procedure for a one-off prescription as it is for all the repeat prescriptions which make up about 80% of the total written. A lot of paper and time are involved and there are many chances for errors to be made along the way.

The paper forms then have to be collected by the patient or pharmacy staff and taken to the dispensary. After the medicine has been supplied to the patient the forms have to be endorsed, sorted and filed then packed up and posted on to the pricing division of the Business Services Authority where the costs and other data are gathered for the NHS. Almost all of this work is still done by hand. Some time later the payment to reimburse the pharmacy for the cost of medicines or equipment supplied and the dispensing fees is sent to the pharmacy.

The new system will be phased in by two stages. This first stage will run the paper and electronic versions together. The new paper prescription forms have a bar-code to be read at the pharmacy. This will download the electronic version onto the dispenser's computer screen. The medicine will be dispensed and supplied to the patient as happens at present and the electronic record passed to the pricing authority for payment.

Later in stage two the paper form will be almost totally eliminated. The patient will be able to direct their prescription to the pharmacy of their choice to be ready for collection at their convenience or delivery where available. Alternatively the patient may be given a bar-coded token to take to any pharmacy which will then be able to download the relevant prescription and dispense it.

So, one might ask, apart from reducing the amount of paper and printer ink what are the main advantages?

When fully implemented EPS should reduce the number of unclear and illegible prescriptions which can lead to the wrong items being dispensed with obvious danger to patients and also allow instant cancellation of items no longer thought clinically appropriate.

At present, medicines no longer used often stay on the patient's record at the doctor's surgery and may be accidentally prescribed causing confusion. There is always the danger that some paper forms will get lost and unfortunately there are some people who try to cheat the system.

Electronic systems could allow the pharmacies to plan their workflow and stock control more effectively so as to have everything ready for collection by or delivery to the patient. This would in turn reduce their waiting time and relieve the patients or pharmacy staff of the need to collect the paper forms from the surgery. Mercifully for all of us, handwritten prescriptions should virtually disappear for ever.

It is hoped that by eliminating the need for re-entering prescription information on each occasion the supply is ordered, more time will be saved and errors avoided. Finally, by not having to sort and send the paper forms at the end of each month the system would allow faster and more accurate processing of the prescription by the pricing authority.

The main disadvantages are in the cost of buying and installing all the new equipment and training staff to use it. All pharmacists, for example, have to be provided with a smart card to access the system. Patient record confidentiality as always is most important.

There will inevitably be some hitches along the way particularly as not all surgeries or pharmacies will be at the same stage at the same time. Also it has to be said that the introduction of new computer systems by government departments usually costs a lot more and takes longer than planned. The new service should eventually benefit the patient by providing a more convenient, efficient and, most importantly, safer supply of their medication.

18

There are some pharmacies that I enjoy returning to over and over again. In spite of the way Alice and her colleagues had coerced me into doing that long walk over the Shropshire hills, I was pleased when a message on my answering machine took me back to Shrewsbury. I was greeted with a nice cup of coffee and a set of those photos taken at the start of the walk. They confirmed my worried look at the time and the ladies in the pharmacy were still laughing at my walking efforts when the telephone rang. Alice picked it up.

'Oh no!,' I heard her gasp. The laughter stopped. 'I'll put you on to the pharmacist.' She turned to me and put her hand over the mouthpiece. 'It's my sister,' she said, her eyes wide open in fear. 'She's got a needle stick injury. Can you speak to her?'

Alice's sister, Carol, was a very agitated young woman who, I discovered, worked as a volunteer in a charity shop. She had been given the job of sorting out a shoe box full of odds and ends which had been left with some other items. At first glance, the contents seemed to consist of small items of jewellery and bric-a-brac, that sort of thing.

Without thinking she had poked her finger into the box and started to sift through these various bits and pieces. That was when she discovered that someone had left some hypodermic needles in the bottom of the box. One of them pricked her finger. This is known medically as a needle-stick injury.

Ideally of course and with the benefit of hindsight she should not have trusted the contents of that box to be harmless. Tipping the lot out into a tray of some sort before sifting through it while wearing thick gloves would have avoided a visit to the hospital, having to undergo tests and several months of worry. In an unguarded moment she had put herself into a dangerous situation.

There are many quite normal and legal reasons why people use needles and syringes of course. Diabetics are the most likely people to do so in the community and they will have been trained to dispose of their needles and syringes safely. Indeed special sealed containers called 'Sharpsboxes' are freely provided on prescription nowadays for them to do so. Unfortunately, in this case the needles had been discarded irresponsibly.

Carol's first panic-stricken thought was that the needles may have been used by a drug abuser. Such people might share injection equipment and the needles could therefore have been contaminated with a variety of diseases such as Hepatitis or even HIV (Human Immunodeficiency Virus) which can lead to AIDS (Acquired Immune Deficiency Syndrome). Needle-stick injuries of this sort can transmit these diseases to an innocent victim.

Carol had been told that there are tests available which will confirm whether one has been infected with HIV or AIDS. She had been sent to be tested straightaway but at the clinic the doctor had told her that she would have to wait for the Hepatitis C test as well as taking another test for HIV in three months time. The doctor hadn't explained why and she was terribly worried.

Testing for Hepatitis C presents a different problem to the tests for other infections. Hepatitis C is a viral infection which mainly affects the liver and is the leading cause of chronic liver disease worldwide. The World Health Organization estimates there are around 170 million people infected with this virus. In the UK the number of victims is thought to be somewhere between 200,000 and 500,000 people. Many of them just don't know if they are infected or not.

The Hepatitis C virus can be transmitted in various ways, by intranasal cocaine use, from mother to baby (perinatal) or by sexual exposure to an infected partner or partners. However it is also transmitted via blood and blood products.

Acupuncture and tattooing are known to be possible routes of infection, along with needle-stick injuries. Blood donations have been screened for the virus in the UK since 1991 although anyone who received a blood transfusion in the UK prior to 1991 or in a country where blood screening is not always carried out could also be at risk.

The other main method of transmission nowadays is through the reuse or sharing of needles and syringes by intravenous drug users. Unlike Hepatitis A and Hepatitis B, no vaccine is currently available to protect anyone against the problems brought by Hepatitis C.

Patients suspected of having Hepatitis C viral infection should have a serological test that detects antibodies to the virus. This is known as the anti-HCV test. It can take up to three months until the levels of the antibodies are high enough to be detected. This will be a worrying time for the patient and his or her family.

A patient who tests positive for Hepatitis C antibodies will have a further test, HCV-RNA, which indicates viraemia (the presence of viruses in the blood). The HCV-RNA can also be used to monitor treatment to predict the response to therapy. These predictions will also be helped by genotyping the virus.

Six main Hepatitis C virus genotypes have been identified so far. Type 1 is the most prevalent in the western world and accounts for about half the cases in the UK. Types 2 and 3 have been treated with most success.

Many patients will not initially show any symptoms of the infection and some will recover spontaneously but around 85% of those infected with the virus will subsequently develop chronic infection. It may take up to 50 years for the disease to progress and the severity of liver damage varies greatly.

The early symptoms, if present at all, are usually non-specific and may include fatigue, poor appetite, jaundice and flu-like symptoms. This stage of the disease may last for many years. Cirrhosis will develop in about 20% of infected patients over the next 20 to 25 years. This may progress to end-stage liver disease or primary liver cancer.

High alcohol intake and other forms of drug abuse are the other primary causes of cirrhosis. An alcoholic drug abuser with Hepatitis C infection is particularly vulnerable. Long term infection with Hepatitis C often results in the need for a liver transplant. This condition is the most common reason for liver transplantation in Europe and North America.

Treatment for Hepatitis C is available nowadays and hopefully will become more effective as and when further research is carried out. The success rates vary and depend on the patient's general health and the type of virus found. Half of those treated could expect to be significantly helped.

The two main drugs used are pegylated interferon and ribavirin. Sometimes both are used together and treatment will last up to twelve months. There are some possible side effects. Most commonly these might include headaches, tiredness, aches and nausea. Sometimes depression, anaemia, itching and skin rashes might be a problem. In all cases specialists will discuss the treatment available and whether it is appropriate for the patient.

Carol had to wait for three months before she could take the first test for Hepatitis C. Much to her relief it proved to be negative as were her other tests and she called into the pharmacy to tell them the good news. Alice passed her message on to me. Her sister was very fortunate indeed.

Answering queries and giving advice over the telephone is an important part of our work. The questions are not always as worrying as young Carol's experience but we can often clear up misunderstandings.

A young man called to enquire about antimalarial prophylaxis. The number of such queries increases each year as more and more of us travel to ever more exotic and remote destinations. This chap had a slightly different problem.

It turned out that his parents had moved from Sierra Leone about twenty-five years ago to live and work in the West Midlands. He had been born in Kidderminster and until now had never returned to West Africa. He was going there soon to visit some members of his family and join their celebration of a marriage.

His query was that as he was born of West African parents would he need to take any antimalarial prophylaxis? Someone had told him that he wouldn't need to take anything as he would be immune from malaria because his family came from Africa. Their immunity would have been passed on to him.

Unfortunately this information was wrong. It is a question we get quite often. Sometimes people who have moved to the UK from a malaria risk area just a few years ago believe they are immune if they return home for a short visit. They still need to take prophylaxis just as anyone who is travelling to the area for the first time.

We also point out that it is important to reduce the risk of getting bitten by the malaria carrying mosquitos by using insect repellents, sleeping under nets and covering up exposed skin.

Some people still don't bother to take any precautions at all. Every year travellers bring serious health problems caused by malaria back with them along with their other souvenirs.

*

Even forty years ago most of the traditional compounding and preparation of medicines had disappeared from the average high street pharmacy. As I said, most of that sort of dispensing had gone but happily not all the fun has vanished from our work. Once in a while the opportunity arises to indulge in a little old-fashioned pharmaceutical creativity.

I had been booked to work in a pharmacy at Church End. The drive to work that Thursday took me past the villages of Aymestry and Wigmore, There are some quarries near Aymestry from where lorry loads of rocks and gravel are taken for various building and road projects. A few miles further on, to the west of Wigmore, lies a series of hills known locally as The Rolls.

I have often driven along this rural road and, in my mind at least, planned a big music festival. I imagine building an enormous stage in Glastonbury fashion. There will be thousands of fans camping in the surrounding fields. Huge banners will be flying everywhere to announce that, "Aymestry Rocks and Wigmore Rolls". It is another dream I fear will never come true.

There were many banners and lots of bunting across the streets of Church End when I arrived that morning. An old dead oak tree in a hedge on the approach to the town had been wrapped in strips of red material and another was covered with ribbons and balloons. I wondered, just for a moment, whether all this jollity had been placed there in celebration of my visit. However inside the pharmacy the dispenser, Angie, explained that an arts festival was about to start.

'It will be on today, Friday and all over the bank holiday weekend,' she agreed the display was not in my honour. 'There are various concerts in the church and town hall, poetry readings all over the place, displays of paintings and sculpture put on by local artists and an open air theatre group are performing at the castle.'

The original castle was built, it is said, by Ethelfreda who was a daughter of Alfred the Great. Ethelfreda was also known as the Lady of the Mercians. She built fortresses and helped to recover areas taken by the invading Danes. She must have been quite a girl. Her wooden structure had been situated near to where the Church End pharmacy stands today. It was replaced by a motte and bailey castle during the Norman period but even that had been replaced or rebuilt several times over the intervening centuries.

The present day castle dates from the decade following the English Civil War when it was rebuilt after Oliver Cromwell's army had demolished the medieval one. I had visited the castle and explored the beautiful grounds with my family on several occasions. It was a lovely place, surrounded by woods and hills. The play was to be performed on the big lawn with the front of the castle as the backdrop.

'The first performance is tonight,' Angie told me. 'Some of us are going with a picnic and a bottle or two of wine. If it stays nice and dry it will be a lovely evening. Last year it was gorgeous. They did Romeo and Juliet then. It was ever so romantic. The sunset, the slowly dimming light, lots of swifts and bats flying around the castle, a fantastic atmosphere. It is a great play and the actors were brilliant too. This year they're doing a medieval tragedy, apparently. Not so romantic perhaps but it should be interesting.'

'The weather forecast for today was quite good,' I commented. 'Let's hope nothing goes wrong.'

'It should be alright,' she replied. 'The actors are having a last rehearsal this afternoon I hear. Then they begin the first performance proper at eight o'clock tonight. I'm really looking forward to it.'

The town was more crowded than I had ever seen it before. The pharmacy was packed all day with customers wanting hay fever remedies, lotions for sun protection and films as well as all the usual queries and requests. The dispensary was busy with the prescriptions that always pile in when the patients realise that a bank holiday is imminent. They seem to forget that we'll only be closed for one day, on the Monday, but they all need to have their next month's supplies now, straightaway. "Just in case" is an expression that everyone seems to use at times like these.

It was about half past four in the afternoon when a commotion in the shop caused me to look up. A flushed and very excited young woman was pushing her way through the throng of customers. She carried a large canvas bag over one shoulder and gripped a clipboard full of papers as if her life depended upon it. The other customers shouted and pushed back but she seemed desperate to reach the dispensary counter and when she arrived, panting, almost collapsed across it.

'Quick!,' she gasped, her face was all red and sweaty, her hair all over the place and her chest heaving. 'I need some blood!'

'What?' I stepped back in surprise and several customers edged further away from her. Angie's eyes opened wide and I'm sure my mouth dropped open too.

'Fake blood!' she shouted as if she were dealing with an idiot. 'We need some fake blood for the play!'

She was getting her breath back by now and started to calm down a little but she still had that look of panic in her eyes.

'I don't think we have any blood here, fake or otherwise,' I said, still trying to get a grip on the situation.

'Can't you make some?' she demanded. 'Haven't you got anything you can make some with?'

Well that was a new one on me and I couldn't think of a solution to the problem off the top of my head. The woman calmed down a bit more and began to explain her problem.

The play to be performed at the castle had a sword fight in one scene where one actor killed another. The director of the play had decided that he wanted the triumphant actor to kneel down by his now dead opponent and then, while making his next speech, raise his sword high above his head. Vertically, she added, like Excaliber and the Lady of the Lake. The dead man's blood was to run down the sword blade, across his killer's hand then down the sleeve of his shirt. Angie shuddered.

'We brought a large bottle of special fake blood with us,' the woman explained that she was responsible for all of the costumes and props used in the performance. 'During the last run through this afternoon someone knocked the bottle off a table and cracked open the stopper.'

Her precious blood, the only bottle of fake blood it seemed for miles around, had seeped into the ground unnoticed. The director had exploded with rage. A great scene ruined, he'd screamed at her when she'd confessed, as if she broken it on purpose. Then he'd ordered the young woman, by now in tears, to find something to replace his blood. Or, he'd stated viciously, he would use hers! We sat the poor woman down and Angie went to make her a cup of tea.

'How much of the stuff will you want?' I asked a short time later as I searched along the stockroom shelves for anything that might be of use.

'About a pint would do, more if you can make it. In case I can't find any for tomorrow's or the weekend's perfomances. We don't need gallons of the stuff, it won't be splashed all over the place but there needs to be enough to show what's going on. The audience won't see a few drops. It needs to ooze down the sword when its held up, sort of gloopy like.'

'Gloopy,' I muttered desperately as I searched among the bottles of cough linctus and stomach mixtures. My mind went back to that cellar in Barnsgrove where, years ago, Amy and I had rummaged through all those dusty old bottles and jars. There would have been loads of gloopy things down there I thought and then wondered what Amy was up to now.

'Gloopy you said. Viscous? oily? syrupy?' The words mixed themselves in my mind as if in a thesaurus. I found a winchester of Syrup BP and a plastic bottle half full of arachis oil. Perhaps a mixture of the two would be gloopy enough.

I reached for the largest glass measure we had and poured some syrup into it then added the oil gradually and stirred. I tried adding varying amounts of water as well but it didn't look right. I went back to the syrup and oil alone. By pouring the stuff from one measure to another I adjusted what I began to think of as the gloopiness factor. The young woman watched every movement and decided at last that we had the required oozing material. She started to look a little less panicky.

'It needs to be red,' she said unnecessarily.

'Yes it would!' I went along the shelves again. 'The only red colour I could make in here would come from a solution of amaranth,' I muttered to myself. 'But will that be the right red?'

I added a few drops of the amaranth solution to a sample of my blood mixture, then a few more, and another one.

'It isn't quite right,' she said, far too critically, I thought, given her desperate circumstances. 'It looks too red.'

'Food colouring,' I said. 'We need to try a few food colours. Blue perhaps, or maybe green, or yellow. Added to that red it might look more realistic.'

'I'll go and get some from that supermarket across the road,' the woman groped in her bag and took out a £20 note. She headed for the door at a good speed, scattering the customers as she went.

After some further experimentation with various food colourings we came up with a solution of nasty gory-looking suitably gloopy fake blood.

Angie went to the play that night and told me when I returned some weeks later that our blood was very effective. I suppose it was more cooking creativity than pharmaceutical but it turned out to be good fun. She also told me that another pharmacist had mentioned that chocolate sauce made a good substitute for blood but that was only of any use in the old black and white Hollywood movies.

So if I ever come across anyone making a black and white film I'll be better prepared. You learn something new every day. A whole new experience gained that I have will probably never have another cause to use.

19

I have spent most of my career as a pharmacist, especially since becoming a locum pharmacist, working in the counties of Worcestershire, Herefordshire, Shropshire, Gloucestershire, Powys and Gwent. Much of my home area is known as the Marches which means borderlands.

William the Conquerer granted land along the Welsh border to his fellow Normans. These men became known as the Marcher Lords and they administered what was in effect a buffer between England and what they called the troublesome Welsh. They didn't get it all their own way of course and Welshmen like Owain Glendwyr battled against English rule for many years.

Glendwyr set up a Welsh parliament at Machynlleth and was proclaimed Prince of Wales but after a few years spent rampaging up and down the border, his rebellion gradually petered out. He disappeared and then faded from history. No-one knows when he died or where he is buried. Some Welshmen believe he waits hidden in a cave to return when his country needs him.

One of the major features of this now peaceful region is its waterways and the way they link the various towns and cities. The sources of both the river Wye and the river Severn are found on a mountain in mid Wales called Plynlimmon. They rise close together then immediately separate as each begins its journey to the sea.

The Wye flows through mid Wales, Herefordshire and Gwent. It passes through Hay-on-Wye, Hereford, Ross-on-Wye and Monmouth and then flows down a lovely valley past the Forest of Dean to be reunited with the Severn near Chepstow.

The river Severn takes a longer and more leisurely route via Powys, Shropshire, Worcestershire and Gloucestershire. For over two hundred miles the river flows through cities and towns such as Shrewsbury, Worcester, Tewkesbury and Gloucester to the sea. Its estuary was known as the Severn Sea to the sailors who carried merchandise up and down the rivers and across the Bristol Channel.

For many centuries boats have carried people, livestock and merchandise along these rivers. The Severn was navigable up to beyond Shrewsbury at one time. Most of the cargoes were carried to and from the seaports of Bristol and Gloucester.

Raw materials were carried up to the industrial centre of Ironbridge or into the canal system at Worcester and Stourport and on into the workshops of the Black Country. Finished goods were carried back downstream to join the sea-going vessels waiting to export them all over the world.

Similarly on the river Wye, timber and stone were carried from riverside villages and quarries downstream then across the Severn Sea to be exported from the big ports or to be used to build the seawalls along the Somerset shore.

As the railways spread across the country during the 18th and 19th centuries the river trade slowly died away. Hundreds of schooners, barges and lighters were broken up or just left to rot on the riverside. Their rotting timbers can still be found in some places along the river estuary. Nowadays there is only one complete sailing barge, or trow as they were called, in existence and she sits inside a corrugated iron shed in a museum at Ironbridge.

All along the river banks at one time you could find the boatyards where they produced those magnificent vessels but nowadays those few yards who survive do so only by repairing narrow boats and pleasure cruisers.

Noah Thornton was a boatbuilder who came from a long line of such men. His family had been busy building wooden sailing barges for at least two hundred and fifty years. When boats began to be built of fibreglass he gave up. He said that he hated the stuff. That was his story but I was to learn that there was another reason for his retirement.

While still only in his fifties Mr Thornton developed rheumatoid arthritis which brought inflammation, swelling and pain, particularly to his hands. This eventually stopped him from being able to use his beloved tools. Then to cap it all he started to lose his sight.

I heard Mr Thornton's story when I worked for an odd day or two at one of the pharmacies near the river Severn in Gloucestershire. As we worked one afternoon a very pleasant middle-aged lady came to ask if she could speak to the pharmacist. I stepped forward to help. She looked surprised. I explained that I was a locum and that her usual pharmacist was away.

'Oh well I don't know if you can help,' she said. 'It is about my father's medicines.'

'No problem,' I replied. 'Let me just find him on the computer then I can see what he takes. What is his name and address please?'

'It isn't what he's taking actually,' she looked a bit uncertain. 'It's just that he can't open the bottles. These special child-proof tops are too difficult for him. Is there anything you can do about that?'

Since the 1970s we have been obliged to ensure that medicines are supplied in what are properly called re-closable child-resistant containers. Whenever it is possible of course we dispense the prescribed medication in the original manufacturer's pack which will comply with the relevant British Standard but often we have to repack the medicine in a suitable bottle or carton. This is usually done in order to supply the quantity prescribed by the doctor where that amount isn't the one available in the original pack. Any new bottle we have to use will be fitted with a child-resistant cap.

The caps were introduced in an attempt to reduce the number of children who died or were injured after taking medicines they shouldn't have taken. Often they thought the brightly coloured tablets were sweets and swallowed as many as they could before being found out. Accident and emergency units recorded many instances of this problem and numbers of children died in spite of their efforts.

Most people are sensible enough to keep their medication locked up or at least well out of reach of children but some of them are not so bright, and some folk just forget the children are around. They might put their tablets down for a few minutes without thinking that their children or grandchildren could pick them up.

While it is certainly a fact that the use of child-resistant containers has helped to reduce the number of deaths of children, there are many adults who find the bottles difficult to open as well. Some people have complained that the containers are too resistant to being opened by the elderly patient and not just children.

Mr Thornton's daughter explained that his arthritis was becoming such a problem for him when it came to taking his medication properly that often he felt it was just too much trouble and so didn't take the dose that had been prescribed by his doctor.

The simplest solution was for us to dispense Mr Thornton's medicine in bottles with ordinary tops. It is clearly even more important in this situation to remind people to store their medication away from any visiting children and Mr Thornton's daughter agreed to make sure this was done.

*

One fine morning some months later I walked back into the same pharmacy in Gloucester. Two young dispensing technicians were already hard at work in the dispensary. As they unpacked some trays of stock and stacked the various bottles, boxes and packages on the shelves they chatted to each other in strange accents. One appeared to be acting the part of a country wench and the other a French maid. I coughed to attract their attention as I walked in.

'Hello,' I said as they turned. 'I'm Paul Rodgers, your locum today. I have been here before, some time ago. I expect you've forgotten me.'

They smiled and said hello. They sounded quite normal now, their usual Gloucestershire accents back in place. One of them, Tricia as I recall, offered me a cup of coffee and went off to make it. Her colleague, Sue, carried on checking off the delivery and putting the stock away.

I sorted myself out and prepared to start work as they finished off their unpacking. They soon lapsed back into those odd accents. After a while I just had to ask what they were doing.

'Those accents,' I started. 'I hope you don't mind me asking. Why the rural talk? A farmer's wench? And the other one? A girl in the French Resistance? Or a French maid? Have you two taken up amateur dramatics? Or what?' They laughed and explained.

'We're practicing our talking labels for Mr Thornton,' Tricia grinned. 'One of the other locums told us such things were available and we thought they might help him. So we ordered a few of them to try out. You remember Mr Thornton? His daughter told us he couldn't open the child proof tops because of his arthritis.'

'Ah yes, of course. I do remember him. His daughter asked us to dispense his medicines in ordinary bottles.'

'We've been doing that for a while now but he's also having trouble reading the labels. His daughter says he's gradually going blind. He can see the bottles and boxes alright but can't read which is which or when to take them. He has three lots of similar looking white tablets and even though they're marked differently the markings are quite small and he sometimes mixes them up.

His daughter helps him when she can by putting his tablets out each day in the order he has to take them but we're all worried he might take the wrong ones. Also she might be away on holiday or something. He'd be stuck then .'

'So why the sexy accents?'

'We were thinking we might cheer him up by using a funny accent when we record the labels. We'll make one of each. Sue's doing the French tart one and I'm the country girl. What do you think?'

'As long as he can understand the instructions I don't suppose he'll mind the accent. Perhaps you'd best explain it to his daughter though. You never know what she might think!'

Talking labels have been developed along with various other odd audio gadgets such as talking greetings cards, photograph albums that describe the subjects of the prints and chatty fridge magnets. The idea of the labels is to provide audible guidance in identifying and taking medicines.

They are useful for people who can't read or, if recorded in the patients language, can help those who don't speak English very well if at all. The small device can be clipped onto a standard pack of tablets and by pressing a button on it the message can be played back over and over again when needed.

The message can be recorded by the pharmacist or dispenser to give the name of the patient, a description of the medication, the dosage instructions and any important warnings such as whether to take the medicine after food or that it may cause drowsiness. They are battery powered and last for quite a long time although you can't use them on medicines stored in a fridge. The batteries don't like the cold damp air.

The labels can be re-used and another message recorded to give new details if necessary when medications or doses are changed. The pharmacy had had to buy them in specially as the National Health Service wouldn't pay for such aids. The girls clearly thought that Mr Thornton was worth it.

'We were going to set the things up today if you don't mind,' Tricia said. 'His repeat medicines are due to go out. That's why we're rehearsing.' She paused and glanced at me. 'Also we need a volunteer to deliver the medicines and the labels to Mr Thornton and explain how they work. The boss was going to do it but as she's away this week she asked us to ask you if you would mind doing that for us instead.

'Mr Thornton lives in one of the old streets down by near the docks, not far from the canal. I've got his address here and I could draw you a map to help you to find his place. It wouldn't be far off your way home after work. You'll be going near the docks anyway. We'll all be really grateful.' She thrust out her chest and lapsed into the eager wench accent as she finished her request. How could I refuse?

I found Mr Thornton's house quite easily. A beautifully carved sailing barge decorated the central panel of his wooden front door. I knocked and waited. Tricia had said he was a bit slow to answer some days. After a few minutes I heard him shuffling toward the door. He opened it. I explained the reason for my visit and Mr Thornton invited me in. We went through a hallway into the kitchen passing, as we went, a well crafted model of one of the old sailing barges in a glass case.

'A trow,' he corrected me as we sat down. 'I've just made some tea. Help yourself.'

He pushed a teapot across the table and passed me a mug and a bottle of milk. My explanation about the talking labels didn't take long. He smiled at the girl's attempted accents, saying that he wished he was thirty years younger.

'I'd have given 'em a run for their money,' he laughed then reached out with his arms. 'Not that I could catch 'em or even hold on to 'em now.'

I'd noticed his hands. They were very swollen and inflamed, no wonder he had given up his boatbuilding career. He would have lost much of his ability to grip or guide his tools. I glanced around the room. The kitchen was very neat and tidy with plenty of shelves and a particularly lovely cabinet lining the walls.

Mr Thornton noticed my interest and admitted with some pleasure that he had built all of it himself. An old fashioned cast iron stove crackled away in one corner and as far as I could see the only modern appliances were a toaster and a fridge. The room reminded me of one of those old pictures of the inside of a ship's cabin. All wood panelling, shelves and lockers.

A square table and three chairs filled the middle of the room and drawings of boats shared what wall space was left between the shelves with some family photographs. Two of the sketches showed large wooden boats being launched off a river bank and another had several men working on a barge that was tied up to a quay. The barge's sails were furled and a long tiller stretched over the cabin in the stern. The men were unloading barrels and boxes from the hold as yet another man wheeled the cargo away using a barrow.

'She was a beautiful trow called Severnsprite,' he said. 'Seventy-two foot long, seventeen foot beam. My great-grandfather owned and built her. She traded across the Severn Sea from the Wye to the Somerset shore mostly carrying quarried stone to build the sea walls but sometimes she carried wine from Bristol or even coal from the Forest. My great-grandmother drew the pictures. She was a very good artist in her time. My old dad made the frames much later.'

'You must have inherited your woodworking talent from your ancestors then,' I pointed to the panels and the kitchen cabinet. 'That's a lovely bit of work. And the boatbuilding was in your blood, I reckon. Was that why they christened you Noah?'

'My first name is Alfred,' he smiled. 'My mum's idea. My dad wanted to call me Noah and that's really my middle name. Dad said he wanted me to grow up and be the best boatbuilder in the country. He said a man called Noah could be relied on to build a good ship.' he sighed and looked tired. 'And build her on time. You'll remember old Noah in the bible would have drowned if he hadn't finished his ark in time. Well I tried to live up to that but nobody wants big wooden boats nowadays and I couldn't do the job anyway now. Not like this.'

*

The next day I went to a pharmacy in Colbury. The building had once been a branch of one of the large banks but was now divided into two small old fashioned looking shops. One shop sold second hand books and prints and the other was a pharmacy. Other than making a dividing wall little had been done to update the fittings. Inside the pharmacy the owner had simply installed some secondhand shelf units and a cut down old wooden counter which looked as if it may have come from the original bank.

As I opened the door on arrival I noticed two things. One was that the owner clearly liked big band dance music. A tape or CD was playing in the background. The other thing that caught my eye was the floor. It was a polished parquet floor and the old wooden blocks had what an antique dealer would call "a patina of age". The blocks were certainly old and well walked upon. They were also mostly loose, very few of them were still glued down, and when one walked across them the blocks moved and rattled.

The staff and their regular customers were used to them and probably never noticed the noise they made but to me whenever anyone walked anywhere in the shop it sounded exactly as if they were tap dancing. What with the music and the tapping blocks I had a picture in my mind of one of those old Busby Berkeley routines in the Hollywood movies. I imagined a glamorous chorus line of dancers twirling their feather boas and kicking their legs high above that counter as they sang and danced. Had Fred Astaire and Ginger Rogers waltzed through the doorway I would not have been surprised.

Noah Thornton in his younger days would have sorted out those blocks in no time, I thought to myself as I hummed and shimmied around the dispensary making the blocks rattle to the rhythm of the music.

*

Some weeks later I was walking along the Gloucester to Sharpness canal near the small village of Purton when I came upon one of the places where many of those old wooden ships had been abandoned when their usefulness had gone. The canal is only a few yards from the bank of the river Severn at this point.

About a hundred years ago the canal engineers became worried that the bank of the canal was in danger of collapsing into the river. They arranged to take some unwanted barges, filled them with rubble and then rammed them as high up the bank as possible at high tide. Men with axes then cut holes in the hulls to stop the vessels floating away and more rubble was piled on top. The canal bank was saved.

Over the years many more unwanted hulls were abandoned on the bank. Historians believe that on and beneath that stretch of grass lie the remains of about eighty vessels. I walked among them that afternoon. Most of the remains are just rotting planks or pieces of bows or sterns. The rest has already decomposed or become buried, sinking slowly into the waving grass.

One of the hulks had the remains of a cabin, just a few planks covered in flaking paint and a porthole. I imagined men like Noah's family sitting by a stove inside the cabin on a dark stormy night making plans for their next voyage. There were a few flowers growing among the wrecks almost like wreaths on their graves.

I thought more about Noah and his family that day as I explored the ship's graveyard. They had probably built some of these barges and the one they owned, the one he'd mentioned, could be there.

Some of the broken hulls had names but others were just lumps of wood with large rusty nails and bits of metalwork sticking out. I looked for but didn't see anything that suggested the hulk of Severnsprite, the subject of his drawing, might have been abandoned there.

Noah hadn't said what happened to her and in reality I hoped not to find her in that sad place. The sky was getting darker and I could see a rainstorm coming up the river so I hurried back to my car with the grass swirling around my legs as the wind rose. A sad last resting place for a difficult but fascinating way of life.

20

I always enjoyed my all too infrequent visits to the New Village Pharmacy. You might guess, quite correctly, from the name that this pharmacy was in a small residential area surrounded by luscious countryside. There were woods and farms, small hedge-ringed meadows full of sheep or cows and, in the distance, the misty blue hills that mark the Welsh border. Perhaps the famous poet A E Housman composed his immortal line about "blue remembered hills" in just such a place.

An area of open hillside just outside the village is simply known to everyone as the Common. It is a lovely place to take a walk with or without a dog, to have a picnic or perhaps to play a game of hide and seek with your children. Around the edge of the Common are plantations of conifers mixed with some areas of other species, mainly beech trees. It is a wonderful place to build dens or just lie under a tree and read on a hot day.

There are some scattered houses across the hillside and each appears to have a small orchard of apple, pear or damson trees or grassy paddock. Most of the people who live up there keep a few geese or chickens. One of the staff in the pharmacy, Shirley, had been brought up at her aunt's cottage on the Common and it was she who introduced me to the area and some of its inhabitants.

*

'Good morning Mrs Jones,' Shirley had noticed the woman approaching the pharmacy counter. 'How are you this morning?'

'I've got a prescription to be dispensed,' Mrs Jones looked a little uncomfortable and stood fidgeting as Shirley checked her details. She had a puzzled look on her face as she spoke to Shirley as if she knew her but couldn't remember where from. 'I'll come back in a few minutes, its only a few pills and some sort of lotion. I'm very uncomfortable. The doctor said these would help.'

Shirley brought the prescription form through to the dispensary. She explained that the patient was one of her aunt's neighbours but that she had only lived on the common for a few years. She was still considered an "incomer" and didn't have much to do with the other commoners.

While Mrs Jones was away Shirley dispensed the items and asked me to check her work. Calamine lotion is a rather old-fashioned thing to see on a prescription nowadays but I suppose it is still useful for itchy rashes and allergies. The tablets were a simple antihistamine, again probably for the same condition. I packed the items in a bag and put them ready for collection.

'Is my prescription ready yet?' Mrs Jones was soon back at the counter. 'What are those tablets anyway, the doctor didn't say much. It is a very uncomfortable itch. A bit personal you know.' She scratched her bottom forgetfully.

Shirley explained that she should take one antihistamine tablet a day until the rash or allergy had subsided. They didn't usually cause any drowsiness so that shouldn't be a problem and the pharmacist had checked that it was compatible with her other medication. She mentioned that such rashes may be caused by coming into contact with some irritant or other or maybe from wearing clothes of a different material to what she normally wore or by using a different washing powder or soap or other toiletries.

Mrs Jones grunted irritably and having picked up her medicines left the pharmacy. She was still probably wondering where she had seen Shirley before. When she had gone Shirley burst out laughing.

'Got her!' she said between giggles. 'I thought she was the one.' Seeing my puzzled look she explained.

A few days previously Shirley had visited her aunt up on the Common. She had described the layout of the Common during one of my earlier locum jobs in the pharmacy so I could imagine the scene. The road gives out soon after crossing a cattle grid and only a bumpy track leads on to the cottages and then to a farm beyond.

The view has hardly changed for a hundred years apart from a few cars and the odd satellite dish. It was a very quiet area generally and most of the people apart from Mrs Jones had lived there for many years. They all knew everything about each other. Or so they thought.

During Shirley's visit she had found out that her Aunt Emma had noticed that some of her clothes had been stolen off the washing line in her garden. This had happened twice now, during the night, and both times only certain items had been taken.

'It did seem an odd thing to happen, there's never been any trouble up there before,' Shirley frowned. 'Only her pants and tights were taken. We couldn't think why.' She grinned. 'There was nothing there that you might think was too flighty you know, just her normal Marks and Sparks stuff. I couldn't imagine anyone getting over excited about those. They weren't even particularly new or expensive ones.

'I reported it to the police on my way to work the next morning. They wrote down the details but I didn't think anything would come of it. I suppose they're not likely to be patrolling up there all the time.' Shirley turned to stare out of the shop window.

Mrs Jones was outside, getting into her car, slowly and with a lot of wriggling to get comfortable.

'I don't like to think of anybody wandering around Aunt Emma's garden at night,' she continued. 'So I did something about it myself. I hung out some more clothes that night. A special bait of tights and pants.

'Oh yes,' Shirley's grin was wider than ever. 'A very special pair of pants. Well dusted with itching powder. My brother got me some from that joke shop in town specially. I think Mrs Jones will be scratching her bum for some time, don't you?' She paused as my laughter subsided.

'I wouldn't dream of betraying a patient's confidential medical history of course so I won't say too much to my aunt but I might just let Mrs Jones know that I know what she's been doing. I don't think that particular thief will be stealing anything else from Aunt Emma's clothes line in the future.'

*

The staff who work in pharmacies are in my experience a caring and hard working group of people. Like those who work in any job where they serve the public they take a lot of abuse and, in the main, they take it, turn the other cheek and work on.

Many customers make unfair demands on the pharmacy staff. For example, they often expect, even demand, that their medicines be delivered to their homes for them. The National Health Service certainly doesn't pay anyone to deliver anything to anyone. Any such service is only given by the kindness of the staff involved who often go out of their way in their own time to make deliveries.

The really galling thing is when one arrives at the home of someone who claimed to have no-one to fetch their medication to discover two if not three cars parked outside and a houseful of family members any one of whom could have fetched the items at anytime.

It would be very rare indeed that anyone as nice as Shirley would take revenge on even the most unpleasant customer in any way. Mrs Jones was very much an exception and one could understand why the itching powder was used. In fact, a few weeks later, Shirley showed another side to her character altogether.

*

It was time to go home, the hectic day almost over. Shirley had just fetched her coat and purse from her locker in the staff room when she remembered that she had promised to deliver something to one of their regular patients, an elderly man who lived in Church Close.

'Is this all ready to go for Mr Thorndyke?' she asked. 'Only I did say I'd pop it in to him on my way home.'

'Oh yes dear,' I said looking at the boxes one more time. 'I've checked those. They're fine. All ready to go although I did wonder why you've put various coloured circles round his labels.'

She had started to put the boxes into a bag but, as I spoke, she stopped and arranged them on the workbench.

'That's a new idea we had to help him remember when to take his medication,' she said. 'Mr Thorndyke is a lovely old chap. We used to see him in here quite often but he doesn't get out much nowadays. His daughter usually collects his stuff but she's away on holiday at the moment so I said I'd deliver his medication for him. His place is on my way home so its no trouble.

'The old chap is very wobbly on his feet but his mind is pretty sharp although he does sometimes get confused with time and place. The milk is sometimes put in the cupboard and the teabags in the fridge. That sort of thing. Senior moments some people call them.

'He has been known to forget that someone would call say at lunchtime or that he'd been invited out to tea. His daughter told us that she thinks he sometimes forgets to take his medicine and gets confused over which one to take when so we came up with a plan. Just in case. We don't want him to make any mistakes with his medication especially while she's away.'

'So how do the colours work then?' I asked, still mystified.

'Mr Thorndyke used to be a painter and decorator in his younger days. My aunt used to get him to do work for her. She said he had a brilliant eye for colours, what goes with what and so on. He was a real artist, she reckoned. I remember him coming to decorate my bedroom when I was a little girl and he explained the colour wheel to me, you know, primary colours and all that.

'I remembered him telling me that different colours were important for feelings. Greens for peace and quiet, reds and oranges for excitement or cool creams to relax. I told him I wanted a pink and purple coloured bedroom. I thought it would be elegant and rich, like a princess.

'He had another theory as well. He thought different colours could also mean different times of the day. Pink in the early morning. The pinky light as the sun comes up, he said. Before it gets too bright. Then orange at midday like the bright noon sun. Evenings, he said, would be blue. Getting a darker shade as the night comes.

'I liked that,' Shirley smiled and nodded to herself at the memory. 'I remember asking him what he would see at teatime. He said green, definitely. Like the afternoon tea of lettuce, cress and cucumber sandwiches my aunt used to make for him when he was working at her house.'

She pointed to the items she had placed in a line across the workbench. Each box was clearly marked with a pink, orange, green or dark blue marker pen.

'I've marked his tablet boxes to help him remember which one to take when. Pink for the tablets he should take in the morning, orange to be taken at lunchtime, green at teatime and the dark blue ones last thing at night. I'll explain the plan to him when I deliver them. I don't know if he'll remember our little chats all those years ago but I reckon he'll think I'm another artist. Just like him. What would you say?' I nodded, impressed with her caring.

'Right that's it, I'm off now.' Shirley picked up the four small boxes and slid them into a bag. She carefully attached a copy of what had been ordered and stapled the bag safely shut. We were always particular about sealing the bag so that nothing could fall out and be lost or mixed up with anything else. Most mistakes, it had often been said, were caused by silly things like that or someone not concentrating on what they're doing or forgetting to do something they knew certainly needed to be done.

Shirley headed toward the door with a cheerful. 'See you next time!'

*

Although I didn't realise it at the time, Shirley's colour coded system was an early form of what later came to be known as a Monitored Dosage System. As the number of residential care homes increased in recent years it became apparent that there were problems in the way that medicines were kept and administered. Care homes are often staffed by people with no special training in what medicines do, how they should be stored or the correct way to give them to the residents.

In the early days few records were kept, drugs were easily lost or stolen, the patients could be given the wrong dose or dosed at the wrong time of the day. Several different systems were developed by various companies but each of them sets out to make the administration of medicines safer. Each resident's medication is stored in a sealed cassette which shows what is to be taken, how to take it and at the correct time.

The benefits of a good monitored dosage system were that the carers didn't have to touch the medicine, security was improved, there was less scope for error, the amount of drugs kept in the homes could be reduced and so there was less wastage when doctors changed a resident's medication.

Detailed medication administration record sheets were introduced as well so that the carer noted what was given or even if it was refused. The actual doses taken were easily monitored and, for the care home owner, fewer staff were needed to do the work.

All this effort made life easier for the owners of care homes and safer for their residents but meant a lot of extra work for the dispensers and pharmacists. It was hoped that the National Health Service would pay for this work and all the materials required but much of the extra cost to fund these systems has fallen on the pharmacies themselves.

Then, in March 2004, the government published plans for a new community pharmacy contract which fundamentally and significantly changed the roles and responsibilities of pharmacists throughout the UK.

21

Primary Care Trusts, shortened to PCTs, are responsible for providing services or commissioning those services for the National Health Service in England. There are, as I write this, just over 150 of these bodies and their boundaries in some instances fit in with our counties. They spend around 80% of the huge NHS budget and can set their own priorities within those set by the Department of Health's Strategic Health Authorities.

Your local PCT provides the funding to pay for a range of community health services, covers the cost of running GP's practices and pays the cost of the medicines on your prescriptions. They also commission hospital and mental health services from appropriate NHS hospital trusts or from the private sector. The funds, of course, come from the tax that you and I pay to the Treasury. There are moves to amalgamate some of the trusts and therefore make savings, not least by reducing their staff numbers, in the future.

The Primary Care Trust which covered Herefordshire, the area I most often worked in, organised a meeting for all the contractors, pharmacists and dispensing technicians in the county. The purpose of the meeting, on Wednesday the 16th March 2005, was to inform us about a new contract due to be implemented during the following year.

Each pharmacy has a contract with the NHS to provide the dispensing and other services. Details of this contract tend to be imposed by the Department of Health rather than negotiated in the true sense of the word. Pharmacy is such a weak profession that one often despairs of it.

Dispensing is still, after all these years, just a form of piecework. The pharmacy buys in the necessary stock and then uses that to supply what is ordered on the prescription form. The Health Service later reimburses the pharmacy for the cost of the items supplied and adds a few pence as a dispensing fee. This represents the major part of their income for most dispensaries.

We gathered together in Hereford after a busy day's work. I recall feeling apprehensive and tired in equal measure. Looking around the room I thought again how rarely those people who actually work in pharmacies, even in the same town or city, get together to discuss the myriad of problems and worries they all have.

As a locum pharmacist I have worked in all but two of the pharmacies represented in that room and I knew almost every one of the dispensers present. I had met some of the pharmacists as well but as my work tends to be done when they are absent I rarely see them at work. So many of the people in that room were however complete strangers to one another.

Six people faced us from the front of the room. Each of them was going to describe some part of the new contract. The first to speak was one of the staff from the Primary Care Trust. He began by giving us what he thought was good news.

'The Government is, as you know, throwing millions of extra pounds into the Health Service,' he looked up from his notes and straightened his already immaculately straight tie. His eyes sparkled with enthusiasm as he brushed a particle of dust from his elegant sleeve. He treated us to his best smile before going on. 'Most of this extra money will of course be taken up by

National Health Service pay and pensions.' He paused for the news to sink in.

There was silence from his audience. He looked surprised. I really think he expected to get a rousing cheer from us. Presumably he didn't realise that all pharmacy staff are employees of the owners of the pharmacies represented. The majority of them work for one or other of the large chains or supermarkets. Unlike him we are not, and never have been, directly employed by the National Health Service. None of those extra millions of pounds in pay, perks or pensions would be coming to any of us.

Pharmacists and their staff have become resigned to being treated in this fashion. I have often wondered why we don't get together and stand up for ourselves. The simple fact is that each pharmacist works alone. Even those who work for the same company rarely communicate with each other on a day-to-day basis. Within large companies, of course, the pharmacists have to do what their employers demand.

The central administration of those companies, their head offices, often has no experience of the realities of actually working in a pharmacy. Few of their management people give a second thought to pharmacy's problems. Some of these companies indeed, such as the supermarket chains, treat their pharmacies in just the same way as a bakery or delicatessen.

Opening hours have been extended further and further. Some pharmacies are now open for one hundred hours a week. The twelve, thirteen or even fifteen hour day is quite normal. The pharmacy is there to make as much of a profit as possible with as few staff and other resources used as they can get away with. There is little professional thought or motive in the methods used by these companies.

The few independent pharmacies that are left are just struggling to survive. Most of them sell out to the large groups as soon as the opportunity arises. The opportunities for a young pharmacist to open up or take over a pharmacy are just about non-existent now.

It seems that there is no-one who will stand up for us as a profession. Very occasionally someone tries to organise a stronger body, even a trade union, as they feel the professional organisation, the Royal Pharmaceutical Society of Great Britain, doesn't support pharmacists enough. These attempts are inevitably a waste of time.

Pharmacists appear to be unwilling to co-operate with each other to demand proper, safe working conditions. Someone once said that trying to organise pharmacists is like trying to herd wasps. I can well believe that is true.

At the meeting in Hereford that evening we learned that the new contract would start off by reducing the amount of money that the NHS would pay for dispensing medicines. We were told that we would have to make up the income necessary to keep the pharmacies in business by taking on new roles in addition to everything we do already.

One of the speakers used by the PCT to support their plans that evening was a pharmacy owner from a neighbouring county. He was very enthusiastic about the potential earnings for pharmacies in future and produced a selection of slides showing how his and thus our dreams could be realised. One or two of those present may have believed him but I suspect most of us were more sceptical. I certainly was.

Earning even the same income as under the old contract would involve much more pressure for all of us and I didn't believe any of the employers would provide the extra support staff that would be needed Without those extra staff to release the pharmacists from the dispensary in order to perform these new roles, the strain was going to grow.

A few years later I read in the Pharmaceutical Journal that the very same enthusiastic and, he suggested, highly motivated pharmacist was imprisoned for fiddling the system in order to increase his income. The majority of us simply struggled on.

*

I got a strong impression that evening that the NHS had decided that most of the dispensing service could be performed by well trained chimpanzees and by cutting their banana ration they could cut the budget too. Presumably this was deemed to be necessary so that they could increase their own pay, perks and pensions.

Meanwhile, pharmacists should be released from routine dispensing to do some of the work now being carried out by all those expensive doctors. Again saving money for other matters. My old mentor from my days in Barnsgrove nearly forty years ago, Archie Johns, had he been present, would be nodding as he recognised his prophecy coming true. I could imagine his eyebrows dancing across his brow as the emotions took hold.

In fact, many of my colleagues had been looking for new roles for a long time. I knew that some of them found the repetitive nature of dispensing work less than satisfying, but I think few of them realised that they would be doing even more work than ever just to stand still. At least in the business sense.

They would have no time to stand still in future, hardly time to think in fact. Certainly no time for a proper break. Even while performing these new tasks we were still to be held responsible for everything that happened in the dispensary and as well as supervising the medicines supplied over the counter. Pressure in the workplace was to become a much talked about issue before very long.

*

One of the outcomes of allowing each PCT to decide for itself how, when or if to fund their local initiatives is that the services offered to the public vary greatly from place to place across the country. My locum work after 2005 took me to pharmacies in Shropshire, Herefordshire, Worcestershire, Gloucestershire and into Powys. There were many differences in what services were available in the different counties, even in individual towns.

The Welsh system is different to the English one in some ways. For example all prescriptions written and dispensed in Wales were made free of the prescription tax while just over the border we English had to continue paying unless covered by one of the specified exemptions. I have no experience of the methods used in Scotland or Northern Ireland but I would imagine there would be some differences there as well.

Some PCTs have introduced services such as the free morning after pill and schemes to encourage people to give up smoking. The details of the systems and the forms that have to be filled in to gain these services also vary from one PCT to another. Some pharmacy companies are included in the services and some were not, particularly when the new services first started being offered. A pharmacy on one side of the street might offer one service while another across the road did not. It can be very confusing for a locum pharmacist as well as the patient.

*

Oral contraceptive tablets have been available free of charge throughout the NHS for many years but more recently the so-called morning after pill was introduced. More properly known as the hormonal emergency contraceptive pill or, by some practitioners, the post-coital pill, this is a single dose of 1500mg levonorgestrel in one tablet.

The tablet can be taken up to three days after having unprotected sex but the sooner it is taken the more effective it is in preventing pregnancy. By that third day there is at best only a 50:50 chance that it will prevent a pregnancy. If vomiting occurs within three hours of taking the tablet a replacement dose can be taken. Sometimes an anti-emetic to prevent the sickness will be needed.

An alternative to taking this pill is to fit a copper intrauterine device or coil. This has to be fitted by a doctor or suitably trained nurse and can be used up to five days after unprotected sex.

Talking about such matters in a busy pharmacy can be embarrassing for patients and staff alike but fortunately most pharmacies have a quiet area or a consulting room now where one can get some privacy.

*

It was mid-morning on a Saturday when a young woman approached the counter. She looked worried and for some reason waved her mobile phone at me as she arrived.

'I want the morning after pill,' she demanded. 'My friend says I don't have to pay for it. It's free.'

'Yes,' I replied. 'Come into the consulting room and we'll see what we can do.'

'I just want the pill,' she said even more loudly and a couple of elderly ladies backed away down the counter. 'I haven't got time to mess about.'

'Nevertheless I have to run through a checklist with you,' I said firmly while trying to be understanding. She was probably stressed by the situation. 'One of the pharmacy assistants can come as well if you like.' She reluctantly followed me into the consulting room.

'The emergency contraceptive is available free of charge either on a prescription or through this local system set up by the health authority,' I started. 'Or you can buy the tablet over the counter. It costs about twenty-two pounds. If you want the free service we have to fill in this form for the Primary Care Trust.'

She rolled her eyes and grunted. I put the necessary form down and offered her a seat. I explained about needing to take the tablet within seventy-two hours of unprotected sex.

'So I have to ask you this,' I said. 'When did you have unprotected sex?'

'Um, I'm not exactly sure,' she answered and looked a little sheepish. 'I went out with some of my friends last night. One of them just phoned me this morning and said that I went off with one of the blokes we met last night. I suppose I'd had a lot to drink at a nightclub.' She looked even more self-conscious. 'My friend says that this morning he's telling everybody we had sex. I can't remember if we did or not. I must have been drunk' She looked close to tears. All her earlier cockiness had gone.

We filled in the rest of the form together and, as all the conditions were fulfilled and she seemed to be within the seventy-two hour limit, I supplied her tablet. In fact she swallowed it right there with a glass of water. She looked more relieved when she thought we were done but I had to go on with the explanation.

'The emergency pill usually works alright but it won't give you any future protection. You can go to your doctor or the family planning clinic to get the normal contraceptive pills. Or make sure your partner uses a condom if you prefer. If your next period is very different from normal or you miss it altogether you should see your doctor anyway. OK? Promise?' She nodded. I had to give her one more bit of advice.

'The pill won't protect you from sexually transmitted diseases either. So if you get an abnormal discharge or any pain or even if you're not sure, you must go to your doctor. There is an infection called chlamydia which is very commonly caught nowadays. You can take a test for that.

'Also, unprotected sex leaves you at risk of getting other diseases like gonorrhoea, syphilis, HIV which could lead to AIDS so please see your doctor. Some of them like HIV and

Hepatitis C may not show up for several weeks. It would be a good idea to use a condom anyway in future. It is the best way to avoid catching sexually transmitted diseases.' She looked a bit shaken but nodded again.

*

A few days later I was in another pharmacy in another county with a different Primary Care Trust and different systems. The pharmacy was inside one of the large supermarkets. The company had decided not to take part in an initiative designed to supply free emergency contraception yet. Here the patient only had two choices. They had to get a prescription from their doctor or buy the morning after pill over the counter.

I had been on duty for barely twenty minutes when a man of about fifty came up to ask to speak to me. He wanted the morning after pill for his daughter. She had told her mother what had happened and the mother had phoned him at work and told him to come and get the necessary tablet.

I explained the situation about the free prescription versus the over the counter purchase and told him the price, twenty-two pounds. Also I explained that I would have to speak to his daughter to ensure the supply was appropriate. I had to check that she was within the time limits and she wasn't taking any other medicine that might interfere with it working and so on. He muttered something about sending her in and walked off.

About an hour later the young woman arrived and explained who she was. I went through the protocol, as we call it, with her. She met all the conditions and said that she was going to pay for the pill rather than wait for her family doctor to write a prescription.

'Dad said to buy the thing and take it as soon as possible,' she said and offered her debit card as I handed her the pack. 'Can I have some water please? I think I should take it now.'

I fetched her a glass of water and watched as she removed the tablet from its foil strip and swallowed it. One of the pharmacy assistants meanwhile rang up the sale and began to process the card. Several failed attempts later we decided that the card wasn't going to work.

'Have you got any other form of payment?' the assistant asked. The girl shook her head. We all looked at one another. The girl had swallowed the tablet, we couldn't get it back. The assistant glared at me for letting her take the tablet without paying for it first and I didn't know what to do next.

'Can you get some money from your father? Does he work nearby?' I asked desperately. The girl smiled at last.

'I'll try,' she said and set off down the shop at a good speed.

'That's the last we've seen of her,' the pharmacy assistant snarled. 'You'll have to explain why the till is twenty-two pounds out to the store manager. She slammed the till drawer shut and stalked away.

A few supermarket managers take the trouble to find out about their pharmacies. Some of them make an effort to introduce themselves to any locums and one or two seem quite helpful. The majority of them do not bother. This particular store manager and I had met, I might say clashed, before. He wasn't going to like my explanation.

When a locum spends a day in a pharmacy he or she fills in a claim form or hands over an invoice in order to be paid. This will hopefully be processed through their head office and, again hopefully, payment will eventually arrive. Sometimes I've had to chase up slow payers and once in while fight quite hard to get my due.

In most large companies like the supermarkets one has to get the signature of one of the management team to authorise one's claim. It sounds simple enough. In practice many of the supermarket managers think we are just there to take the money.

Getting paid is nice of course, very nice, but most of us do earn it as well.

The first time this particular store manager and I met was a few weeks previous to this day when I asked him to sign my claim.

'I suppose so,' he grunted and read my details. He did sign the form but went on to add as he handed it back. 'I wonder if you people are worth all this sometimes. You've got a cushy job.'

I pointed out that without a pharmacist on duty he would have to close the pharmacy. This would inconvenience his customers as well as lose money from his takings.

'On the other hand,' I added pointedly. 'If you go home or weren't here one day the place will carry on quite normally.' I waited until he'd gone before finishing off with, 'Probably better!'

On another occasion he refused to supply anyone to cover a pharmacy assistant who had gone off sick and even tried to take the one remaining girl away to man one of his checkouts.

Fortunately for all concerned, and especially for me, the young lady with the useless debit card came back with some cash later in the morning. Bless her!

22

One of the most popular of the new services offered by pharmacies in recent years has been the smoking cessation programme. Smoking causes an enormous amount of ill health and death as we all know. It also has huge consequences for the cost of maintaining the National Health Service.

The government has tried to reduce smoking by increasing taxes and restricting advertising but still many people start smoking each year and large numbers find it too difficult to give up the dreadful weed without some help even when they want to do so.

Some researchers have found that you are at least four times more likely to succeed in your attempt to stop smoking if you have regular on-going personal support along with some form of nicotine replacement therapy. The community pharmacy is the major supply point for these products where they can be sold over the counter, dispensed on prescription as well as supplied under the local Primary Care Trust supported initiatives.

We found that a lot of patches and such items were wasted when prescribed by doctors as the patient didn't normally have any other support. After the first few weeks or so they invariably gave up their attempt. As some doctors insisted on prescribing a whole course of patches or gum on one prescription, most of the medication was just thrown away.

The NHS still had to pay for the stuff even though it wasn't used. Also, it costs the NHS a lot more for a doctor to see a patient than for a pharmacist to do the same job. We can see them more quickly and usually at times more convenient to them too. The PCTs were very keen for smoking cessation programmes to be set up in pharmacies, thereby diverting such patients away from the doctor's surgeries.

Nicotine replacement therapy is available in many forms the most popular of which are as patches and chewing gum. Sublingual (under the tongue) tablets, nasal sprays or oral inhalers are also used. For many people the problem they face in giving up comes in many forms as well. As well as being addicted to the nicotine in their cigarettes, they find it difficult to break the habitual actions of just handling a cigarette. Many of them find it awkward being with other friends who smoke and offer their cigarettes around. Many of those who want to quit smoking say that they just don't know what to do with their hands when they no longer have a cigarette to hold.

The initial wish to quit has to come from the patient. No power on earth will stop the dedicated smoker who wants to carry on. Only death will stop some of them. Having decided to stop they have several choices. Apart from the pharmacy-led programmes smokers can choose to buy the nicotine replacement of their choice or get a prescription from their doctor and simply decide on a day to start and get on with it. This does work for some people but far more of them come to speak to their pharmacist. A young man called James Lewis was one of the first to arrive after the smoking cessation programme started.

'I want to learn to drive and buy a car,' was almost his first sentence as we settled down for a chat in the consulting room. 'I've worked out that I spend about forty pounds a week on cigarettes. That's terrible! I didn't realise I spent that much until I added it all up. My mum said I could get some driving lessons with that and maybe save some towards a car.'

'That's as good a reason as any to quit,' I nodded. I suppose I hoped that he might have thought about his health and the way that smoking would affect it but any reason is good enough for me.

James was typical of many young lads in that he'd started smoking secretly at school and just carried on because his mates did. Like many men he appeared to have a dread of going to see his doctor. In fact he didn't seem to know who his doctor was, he said he'd have to ask his mum.

He wasn't taking any other medication but he'd heard about the patches and chewing gum and had come into the pharmacy to ask about them. The pharmacy assistant had mentioned that we were starting this new programme and when she said it was a lot cheaper to join it than buy the nicotine replacement products over the counter he was happy to volunteer.

James blew into our carbon monoxide meter, the indicator shot well up the scale and we made a note of the reading on a new record card. He was advised to return each week to have a retest and I promised him that if he stopped smoking that first high figure would gradually drop in line with the fall of the amount of carbon monoxide in his system.

To demonstrate, I took the test myself and as a non-smoker registered almost zero. We decided that he would use patches as he felt his mum wouldn't want to see him chewing gum all the time. Nor, come to that, would his boss like it as he had to meet and talk to customers in his job. He seemed a bright sensible lad and I reckoned he would have every chance of success.

As James was quite a heavy smoker I started him off on the highest dose of patch. He was advised to replace the patch each day, varying the site he used to prevent any skin reactions and return in seven days for his follow-up check and another pack. After a few weeks of the higher dose we would reduce the strength gradually until he was not only a non smoker but also patch-free. And, I suggested, he would have a lot more money in his pocket. He went off to book his first driving lesson.

I didn't go back to that pharmacy for several months but when I did it was to find that James had not only stopped smoking but had passed his driving test. He was also going out with Jenny, the dispenser. A very sensible lad. I reckon he must have been really pleased that he came into the pharmacy that day to ask about nicotine replacement therapy. Later I discovered that he'd done even more. His success had encouraged his father to join the programme as well.

Mr Lewis was a regular customer at the pharmacy. For several years he had been collecting his prescription each month. His medication suggested a high blood pressure combined with a raised level of cholesterol. He was also overweight and usually had to sit down for a few minutes before he left. As Jenny said, diabetes would be his next health problem followed by heart failure.

His future was mapped out in some grim detail and had a lot to do with his smoking habit. She and James had suggested he seek help. He was put on the same programme as the one that James had joined and, when I saw him, had already cut down the strength of his patch to the lowest one available.

The whole family had become healthy eaters and began to take more exercise. Mr Lewis had already lost some weight and Jenny was especially pleased to show me his latest prescription. The doctor had found that his blood pressure was better controlled and had come down to a more acceptable level. He had suggested that they could lower the dose of his medication.

Patients often find that this happens when they quit smoking. Smoking can also affect other drugs so it will be necessary to monitor their medication as they stop smoking. Another benefit is the money saved for the Health Service as well. Instead of paying millions of pounds to treat smoking related diseases we can use the funds to start solving other health problems instead. Everyone is a winner, as they say, except the tobacco companies.

*

Alongside the services funded by the Health Service through the PCTs, like smoking cessation, some pharmacies also set up other schemes. The NHS doesn't always pay for all of these new initiatives. It is left to the pharmacies themselves to find the funds if necessary.

There are pharmacies where you can be tested for diabetes, have a check on your blood pressure and a blood test to determine your cholesterol levels. Some places offer a test to detect chlamydia and others are looking into the provision of tests for Hepatitis C. These services vary from place to place so the far-ranging locum has to be prepared for whatever he finds.

It was a chilly Friday afternoon when Alan Willis came into the pharmacy. He was one of the regular patients who collected their medication each month and sometimes stopped for a while to chat up Heather, the dispenser. I looked up to see a pleasant man of around fifty years of age smiling at Heather as she handed over the bag of his various tablets. He loitered by the counter and she asked him how he was.

'Oh not so bad,' he said then hesitated. He rolled up his sleeve and thrust his arm out across the counter. 'What do think of these bruises? I don't know what I've done to get them.'

'I ask the pharmacist,' Heather turned to me and looked worried. 'They look nasty,' she whispered.

The bruises did indeed look nasty. They appeared to be spreading in several places along his arm as if the tissue beneath the skin was itself bleeding. Then he pulled up his trouser leg to show me a large bruise on his calf as well.

'Hmm, I see what you mean,' I was making time for myself and pressed one of the bruises gently. 'You say you

219

haven't injured yourself at all? No falls or knocks?' He shook his head. I opened the prescription bag. 'What medicines do you take? Anything else apart from these tablets?'

The bag contained digoxin tablets for the heart, bendroflumethiazide which was probably for raised blood pressure and simvastatin to lower his cholesterol. I didn't see any of those causing bruises like the ones on his arm. I had realised that he was bleeding under the skin and was thinking of any possible drug reaction.

'No,' he said. 'Except the warfarin.'

'Warfarin?' I heard Heather ask. She had been checking his patient medication record while I was speaking to him. 'We haven't ever dispensed warfarin for you. Have you had them from somewhere else?'

'From the hospital,' he nodded. 'I had to go in for a few days recently for an operation and they put me on warfarin. I've got to go back and have regular blood tests as well. In fact, I'm on my way there now. I thought I'd pick up these medicines in case I'm not back before you close.'

'That might explain the bruises,' I said. 'They will almost certainly have to adjust your dose of warfarin. I reckon you might be taking too high a dose and instead of just preventing blood clots to form its actually going too far and making you bleed. Make sure you show them your bruises at the hospital.' He thanked us and headed for the door then turned round again.

'Oh, and I had some antibiotics and painkillers from the dentist as well. I had to go over to Worcester to see him so I got the prescription dispensed there as well. Would that make a difference?'

'It might,' I replied. 'Some antibiotics can interact with warfarin. Erythomycin for example, can increase the effect of warfarin. So can some painkillers. Make sure you tell all this to the staff at the hospital. It might be that it is only a temporary increase in effect. You might get back to your proper warfarin level when you stop taking the antibiotic and painkiller.'

I was also wishing that we could have comprehensive records for our patients.

*

Just a couple of weeks later I found myself working in a pharmacy which offered INR testing on the premises. INR stands for International Standardised Ratio and is the full title given to the results obtained when monitoring the effects of taking warfarin.

Warfarin is taken for its anticoagulant effect. It is used to treat abnormal or undesired clotting of the blood in for example deep vein thrombosis or pulmonary embolism. The drug may also be used after fitting artificial heart valves and for patients with atrial fibrillation. It keeps the blood circulating properly and so helps to reduce the risk of having a stroke.

The treatment is usually started when a patient is in hospital and blood tests are regularly taken to make sure the dose taken is the correct one. There are four different strengths of warfarin tablets and they are used in combination to get the right level of anticoagulant activity.

A small blood sample is taken by pricking the patient's finger and this is placed on a test strip. The strip is fed into a special meter which calculates the time taken for the blood to clot and this is expressed as the INR. The figure will alter as the doctor adjusts the dose of warfarin. The dose is adjusted until the correct clotting time or INR target is reached.

Too little warfarin will mean that the blood clots too quickly and may block the blood vessels and so kill the patient. Too much warfarin and the blood won't clot properly and the patient may bleed to death. Achieving the correct INR level is obviously vital.

That earlier patient, Mr Willis, had taken his INR tests at the hospital and they would adjust the dose of warfarin as it became necessary. Taking a medicine which increased the effect of the warfarin as Mr Willis seemed to have done would be like taking an overdose of the drug. Therefore, when we saw him, his blood wouldn't clot properly and so began to leak out of his blood vessels to appear like bruises on his skin.

The particular pharmacy I was working in that day was able to offer such a testing service because the technique and equipment needed is now available outside the hospital. The pharmacist had invested a lot of his own time and money to get the project up and running. Also the pharmacist who usually worked there had been trained to do the testing while he worked in the hospital. He was ideally placed to offer this service.

It was much more convenient for the patients to come to the pharmacy rather than go to the hospital for their tests. They usually made a regular appointment to see the pharmacist and didn't have to wait long for the result. In fact the result was available within minutes and the pharmacist was able to adjust the dose of warfarin needed straightaway.

An added advantage which may not be apparent to the patient is that the pharmacy has a more complete record of the patient's medication. In the case of Mr Willis for example, his regular pharmacy knew about his usual medication. His dentist may have recorded the antibiotic and painkiller prescribed but they were dispensed elsewhere and only the hospital and his GP knew about the warfarin. No-one had a complete record of all the drugs he was taking and that is what could have been so dangerous. Mr Willis might easily have bled to death.

It was a happy ending for Mr Willis when his warfarin dose was sorted out at the hospital but sadly that other pharmacy no longer provides an INR testing service. Some months later I returned to find an unused INR meter and some redundant test strips sitting on a shelf. The dispenser filled in the details.

The cost of providing the INR testing service, the test strips, meter and so on had been met by a contract with the Primary Care Trust. It was a splendid example of how the patients could benefit from a simple well organised system while the cost to the NHS, or taxpayer, was kept down to the minimum by utilising a local pharmacist instead of a hospital department.

One of the local doctors found out that he could increase his surgery's income by offering the same system and getting one of his nurses to do the actual testing. The PCT cancelled the pharmacist's contract and now pays the money into the doctor's practice bank account instead.

The new dispensing contract, you may remember, reduced the payments to pharmacy for dispensing and offered new roles for the pharmacists to replace that lost income. You may agree that the new contract or at least its implementation is not always so fair to pharmacists after all.

23

There is nothing quite like our National Health Service in any of the other European countries nor indeed in many parts of the world. Each of those other countries makes some provision for their population to receive medical attention as and when needed of course but none do it as we do. There are also some similarities. The brand names of drugs may differ from one language to another but the training of pharmacists is much the same. Dispensing is dispensing wherever you are but the way we work here is very different.

As the borders of the countries within the European Union have opened up to allow free movement of the people so have the numbers of people moving across them in order to seek employment increased. Pharmacists are no exception to this flow of people looking for something new, somewhere different to explore and new cultures to experience while at the same time hopefully earning some money. Some of these continental pharmacists definitely found a new, strange culture when they moved to Britain.

'We're having a new pharmacist,' Eve said as I settled down to work one morning. 'The company has been recruiting pharmacists in other countries. Poland and Spain mostly I think. We'll be having one of the first to arrive. Her name is Izabella. She's Spanish and starts next week.'

'She'll find it strange, I expect,' I had heard that several companies were searching for new staff abroad. They were hoping to exploit a cheap source of pharmacists who wanted to work over here for a while. 'Presumably she'll be trained somewhere first.'

'Not really,' Eve showed me the letter from head office. 'We haven't had a permanent pharmacist here since Mr Reece left so they're sending her straight to us. I think we'll still be having some of you as locums as well for a couple of weeks to give her chance to settle in.'

'Blimey! She'll need more than a couple of weeks to learn this system. Does she speak good English? Medical-type English? Does she know how to do the job our way?' I could see problems ahead and as I had been booked to work in that pharmacy for several days during the next few weeks, those problems were likely to be mine to deal with.

'I don't know anything about her at all actually,' Eve pursed her lips. 'The area manager told me to look out for a flat for her so I've found one I hope is alright. It isn't far from here, close to where I live, so I can keep an eye on her. We'll just have to take it from there.'

*

Izabella arrived on the following Monday morning an hour or so after me. She was about twenty-two years old, tall with long dark hair and an attractive friendly smile. She introduced herself and apologised for her lack of English. It was, we soon discovered, adequate for ordering a meal as you would on holiday but I wondered how she would communicate with the patients. She would be well trained as a pharmacist, I was sure, and perfectly capable of doing the work in a Spanish pharmacy. But here?

Izabella had never seen an NHS prescription form before her arrival, she had only visited England once as a schoolgirl and had no idea how to use the company's computerised patient records and stock ordering systems. She looked aghast when I mentioned the Drug Tariff at one stage and showed her some of the forms we had to complete.

She looked on in amazement when a patient came in to request a supply of the emergency contraceptive pill. I didn't think until much later that perhaps she might have some religious or conscientious objection to supplying them. Some pharmacists do. We are allowed to refuse a request for this item but we must ensure the patient is directed to another pharmacist who will make the supply.

I should have explained that to her but there were so many things to explain in a short period that some could be easily forgotten. She had so much to learn and then, I suspected, would be left to get on with it as best she could.

'Don't scare her off, don't try to tell her too much at once,' Eve whispered to me at one stage. 'She'll pick it up in time.'

We all tried very hard to help Izabella to settle into the pharmacy. Both I and other locums as well as Eve spent a lot of time explaining the systems to her but she never seemed to get any more confident.

That first morning Eve gave her the key to the flat and directions to find it. Izabella was back in about twenty minutes virtually in tears. She couldn't get in to the flat. The key didn't fit. Eve looked surprised but went to the flat with her to try again. The door opened at once. The poor girl had tried to turn the key the wrong way then panicked and kept trying the same direction. Perhaps locks in Spain are different to ours.

Her lack of English was the real problem. She had no idea what people meant when they described their symptoms or asked advice about their medication. I suppose I would have as much of a problem should I go to work in Spain so I certainly didn't blame her. I do however feel that the company that recruited her should have checked her language ability better before accepting her and made much more of an effort to train her when she first arrived instead of hoping that 'on the job' training was enough.

They didn't take into account the fact that we have to have so much direct contact with the patients. There is no chance to hide away out of sight in the dispensary nowadays. Our patients were unlikely to want to wait while she looked something up in her dictionary. Two months later Izabella went back home, possibly sad, wiser I hope, but probably much relieved.

*

A few months later a Polish pharmacist turned up. Magda had excellent English. She was a little older than Izabella, about twenty-five I'd say, and much more confident. Like Izabella however she had no previous experience of our funny little ways and had many questions. I've lost count of the number of times she rang me and probably others as well to ask us to explain something in the Drug Tariff. As if we understood it all!

Magda could communicate with her patients very well usually although she was caught out by the odd colloquial expression. She rang me up at another pharmacy one day to ask in a whisper, 'What is the old feller'?

I could picture the scene. A man, probably elderly, seeing an attractive young woman, and foreign at that, standing across the counter before him chickened out of using the word penis. Almost certainly he would have asked for some remedy or other with just the barest of detail. Magda had, as we do, tried to get some more information out of him to make sure he was getting the most suitable product.

Presumably Eve and the other staff were all busy with other customers and Magda had no-one else to ask. She had sensibly used her discretion and had gone round to the back of the dispensary out of his hearing to use the phone.

'He says it is sore and itchy,' she whispered in something of a growing panic. 'But what is it?'

For my help in this and other bits of advice the lovely Magda was very grateful. She even bought me a gift. A very Polish gift which gave me a taste of this new Europe.

'What does one do with a jar of Smalec Domowy?' I asked when I'd unwrapped the package Magda gave to me. Later I was to ask 'What is Fasolka? How is Golabki made? What goes into these things?' Later at home my wife and I decided that some tasting sessions were in order.

With the influx of people coming from other parts of Europe to work in the UK, shops have opened in many towns to supply their 'comforts from home'. Some of our supermarkets have also begun to stock these foods.

We started with that gift of a jar of Smalec Domowy from my grateful colleague. Magda's Polish-English dictionary hadn't been much help but I eventually found out that it translates as something like Sandwich Fat. So I thought I'd treat it as dripping and tried smearing it on a thick chunk of bread. Mmm, I thought, moving on ...

There are, we found during our researches, similar recipes from different countries. For example, Golabki which is a Polish food and Holubtsi from the Ukraine, are both cabbage leaves rolled and stuffed with meat or rice. Varenyky (Ukrainian) and Pierogi (Polish) are pastry pockets filled with potato, cheese, saurkraut or cherries or anything you've got handy really, and quite tasty too. Kovbasa is a smoked pork sausage which comes from the Ukraine and Fasolka turned out, to my mind, to be reminiscent of the sort of bean dish we used to produce when we went on camping trips.

We discovered that Nalysnyky are a Ukrainian version of crepes. Another customer in the local Polish Supermarket told me that Ukrainians always claim that crepes are a feeble French attempt at making Nalysnyky! I don't know which is true but they were very nice.

Magda went home for a holiday that summer and brought back some more goodies for us to try. The Piernik Torunski or Torun-style gingerbread men went down well and Szarlotka which is a sort of apple cake was definitely one of my favourites. As long as these Euro-pharmacists bring such things with them, the more who want to come the merrier I say.

*

Magda and, I dare say Izabella, would have been useful to have around when we were inundated with foreign students one summer. A local fruit and vegetable grower had set up lots of polytunnels in his fields and had brought in dozens of caravans. The local people were up in arms as large areas of the countryside disappeared under plastic sheeting and rows of little aluminium boxes.

Those people whose properties overlooked this seething hive of industry formed an action group. Meetings were held, letters written and television crews appeared like wasps around a jam sandwich. The plastic tunnels and caravans remained in place. They were to stay for a few years despite the activity of the neighbouring action groups.

The caravans, it turned out, were needed to house the hundreds of students and other migrant workers who were coming to spend their summer picking the resulting strawberries and other fruit grown inside those plastic tunnels.

Although they came from all parts of Europe the majority of the workers were recruited from countries such as Poland, Ukraine, Croatia and Romania. We soon got used to seeing long lines of them plodding along the road between their caravans and the supermarkets in town. One or two of them brought bicycles and a few hitch lifts but most of them just walked everywhere. I'm sure the supermarkets were so pleased to have all the extra business.

As time went by, buses were organised to carry them and their supplies back and forth but that meant that whereas two or three at a time had wandered into the shops, now crowds of fifty or sixty all arrived at once. They seemed to be a very pleasant bunch as far as I could see. I didn't hear of any troublemakers among them. In fact I reckon they were better behaved than some of the local youngsters.

It was however a little unnerving to see so many of them all at once and that was especially so when a whole crowd turned up in the pharmacy seeking medication or advice. We soon discovered that while most of them could browse the aisles of the supermarkets without any problem and quite a few had a smattering of English, enough to ask for bread and beer for example, very few could explain their medical needs.

*

It was only a small pharmacy that I was working in at that time and suddenly the sales area filled with people. They blocked the sunlight making the dispensary quite dark. I looked out to see a group of about ten or twelve of the young fruit-pickers.

They looked, as usual, very suntanned and healthy, casually dressed and most of them were smiling and laughing. The crowd formed into a loose semi-circle in front of me and pushed one girl forward. Of all the gang she looked the most worried. I assumed she had been chosen to be their spokesperson.

She was stunning girl, fit to be a fashion model at least if not a film star. About 19 or 20 years old I'd say and straightaway I noticed, as you would, her long brown hair with lovely glossy curls, her eyes were dark, a little dull just then I noted although they could clearly sparkle with mischief. Her nose was perfect, her lips looked soft and luscious.

The girl wore little if any makeup, a white T-shirt, shorts and sandals. Her long brown legs seemed to go on for ever. As she approached the counter I became aware of a warm healthy scent of strawberries and life in the open air. Her teeth when she opened her mouth to speak were white and even. I waited to hear what she was going to say.

'Dijareja?' At least that's what it sounded like. Diarrhoea, near enough, I thought and wondered how such a word could sound so lovely coming from those tempting lips. Or why indeed such a lovely creature should ever have to utter such a word let alone suffer the distress of having it served upon her.

'Diarrhoea?' I asked gently. One of her friends mimed the effect of suffering a bout of diarrhoea quite effectively. The girl looked embarrassed and another of the group said something like 'proliv' and the play-acting lad laughed. She fumbled in her bag and took out a small pocket dictionary. Croatian - English, I noticed. She opened the book and pointed to the word Proljev - Diarrhoea. So far so good, I thought.

One of the mnemonics we use in the pharmacy to remind us of the correct ways to deal with such patients uses the word WWHAM. This has nothing to do with that odd singing duo who seemed to be everywhere during the 1980s but stands for; **W**ho is the patient? **W**hat are the symptoms? **H**ow long have you had those symptoms? **A**ny treatment tried so far? and what other **M**edicines does the patient take?

The answers to these questions usually gives us sufficient information to suggest a treatment or to refer the patient to a doctor or hospital as appropriate. The process is much easier to follow if both parties speak the same language.

I led the girl to a quieter end of the counter and as her friends browsed around the shop we used her dictionary to answer the rest of my questions. I was able to suggest a suitable remedy and she left the pharmacy looking a good deal happier than when she came in.

We found ourselves faced with similar situations quite often that summer and invested in a few phrase books of our own for those times when the patient hadn't brought their own. By the time a new batch of youngsters arrived the following summer the staff had made themselves some laminated cards with the most commonly used words in several languages. Another unpaid service, as one of the staff said, but it was a satisfying one as well.

24

One of the main problems that all pharmacists have is finding enough time to get out of the dispensary in order to carry out the new roles demanded of them nowadays by the Health Service and their employers.

Most pharmacies now have a separate consulting area or even a small partitioned off room so that patients can discuss their needs confidentially. However it is difficult to concentrate on advising your patient or checking their understanding of their medication or doing blood tests for cholesterol or diabetes while being constantly interrupted by other matters.

Some pharmacists have tried to get their head office to agree to them having a second pharmacist on duty for a few hours a week. This costs money of course and some companies will not do it but the idea makes perfect sense to me. Late one evening my telephone rang.

'Paul? Is that you?' Jillian, the pharmacist in one of my regular workplaces had a proposition to make. 'Would you be interested in doing half a day regularly, say on Tuesdays?'

I had been thinking of cutting down my workload from the usual five or sometimes six full days a week for a while by that time and doing half a day in a fairly local pharmacy sounded like a good idea. More so in that particular pharmacy as I knew

Jillian had an excellent staff and good sound working practices in place.

'It sounds alright,' I said. 'What have you got in mind? Are you having a half day off now?'

'You must be joking!' Jillian groaned. 'You know what its like everywhere, more and more work and no extra staff. No, believe it or not but I've got head office to agree to me having some help for a few hours a week so that I can do some MURs.'

MURs are Medicine Use Reviews and are intended to offer patients the chance to spend some time with a pharmacist so that any questions about their medication can be explained. Of course patients do have their medication reviewed by their doctor once in a while but it was found that many of them didn't know why they were taking that medicine, what effect it might have and even how and when to take it properly. We also found many patients for example who had problems in actually taking their tablets. Perhaps they couldn't swallow them very easily and didn't know that a soluble or liquid form might be available.

Some people weren't sure what time of the day was best to take their medicines or how to avoid any side effects or even whether to take it regularly or only when required. We can give this advice quite easily if only we have the time to do it. We could also let the doctor know about their problems and ask him to alter the prescription if we carried out an MUR.

These MURs were intended to supplement the doctor's review and help to make more effective use of the patient's medication. It takes time for such questions to be dealt with and Jillian, like everyone else, was trying to find the best way to do it.

'That's a good idea,' I said. 'When do you want me to start doing this half day?'

'Would next Tuesday be alright? I thought perhaps you could be here from something like ten o'clock until four in the afternoon. We could both have a lunch break as well then. Such luxury!'

'Perfect!'

*

Tuesday came and I had the pleasant experience of having a slow relaxed breakfast and even a second cup of tea. I wandered around my garden for a while, sniffing roses and checking my vegetable patch then cleaned myself up and set out. I noticed the traffic on the roads was much less congested than during my usual commute. The school run was long over, everyone else was already at work and the early bird shoppers were out of the way.

'I could easily get used to this,' I remarked to Lynne, the dispenser, as I wandered in to work just before ten o'clock.

'Don't get too relaxed,' she warned. 'We've had a load of prescriptions in for one of the residential homes. We've done the dispensing and they're all ready to be checked. If you can get that done before lunchtime please, someone from the home is going to come and collect all of their medication about two o'clock.'

'Right I'll make a start. Is Jillian around?'

'She's in the consulting room with the first MUR patient. He was a few minutes early but she carried on anyway.' Lynne passed me the first of the cassettes of medication for the home to check. 'Have a look at that note attached to this prescription,' she added.

Many pharmacies dispense the medication for those residents of care homes into special cassettes these days. The idea is for all the medicines to be set out so that the staff at the home can issue the doses accurately to the relevant patient and keep a proper record of what was given on a record sheet. In most systems each dose is placed in a blister which is identified to a particular time as well as the patient. Therefore, hopefully, no doses are missed or indeed doubled up and the medicines are used safely.

The medicines are dispensed from a prescription issued by the patient's doctor at the request of the person in charge at the residential home. This happens each week or each month depending on the system and the doctor may, if they wish, change the dose or even stop one medicine and start another.

The prescription that Lynne handed to me had two sticky notes attached to it. The first message appeared to come from someone at the care home and read, 'Please can you increase Elsie Davidson's quetiapine tablets to 200 mg twice a day. She is still throwing bananas at the staff.' Quetiapine is used to control conditions like schizophrenia.

The doctor had added the second note himself. 'I'll review Elsie's tablets when I see her next month. In the meantime it would be better to stop giving her bananas.' I looked at Lyn and she laughed.

'I suppose we are expected to pass that on to whoever collects the medicines. They will be pleased!'

About three quarters of an hour later Jillian came out of the consulting room and saw her patient off. She spread several forms across the workbench to check she had all the details down then filed them into a large but otherwise empty folder.

'One down and only three hundred and ninety-nine to go,' she said with a nervous laugh. 'It took me a lot longer to do than I thought it would. That patient had been taking medication for asthma and appeared to be doing well but it all takes time to go through it all. I wanted to make sure he was using his inhalers properly.' She took out another set of forms ready for her next patient and continued.

'Head office want four hundred MURs done before the end of the year so they can claim the maximum amount of money for doing them. That would be an average of about eight a week throughout the year. I'm a bit late starting so I'll have to try and catch up.'

'How many patients have you got lined up for today?' I asked.

'Only eight I'm afraid. I went through our regular patient's files and picked out those I thought might benefit most from the review. Those patients who have several different medicines or complicated dosages, you know? During the last few days I've actually asked twenty-three people if they'd be interested in having a review but only eight of them either could or wanted to come today.

'I've started making appointments for more patients next week. Hopefully the numbers will build up. Assuming I won't be able to do any MURs around Christmas time or if anyone's on holiday, I need to fit in more than eight a week. I think this Tuesday half day from you will be a great help if you can keep doing it.'

'It suits me very well,' I said and added. 'I've done the training for MURs as well and am qualified to do them but I haven't had the chance to actually do one yet. I'm accredited with all the PCTs in this area but in most of pharmacies I go to I'm the only pharmacist there.

'Very often they're short of other staff as well. There was no dispenser at all in three of the five pharmacies I worked in last week. There's no way you can do MURs when its like that. I sometimes wonder why we bother to take the training courses at all you know.'

'I said exactly that to my dad once. He's a teacher, or was. He's a retired headmaster actually,' Jillian laughed. 'He told me a story from ancient Greek history. Apparently, Euclid had a pupil who asked him what was the use of the maths he was learning. The great mathematician apparently turned to his slave and said, "Give the boy a coin, since he desires to profit from all that he learns". Then he kicked the lad out of his class.'

'That's very comforting, thank you,' I went back to checking that pile of prescriptions.

'And this is my next patient, I think. Hello Mr Williams,' she picked up her papers and led the man into to the consulting room. I heard her start by saying 'Thank you for coming. So how are you today?'

*

As there were two of us pharmacists in the pharmacy that day we had the luxury of being able to take a proper break at lunchtime. We tossed a coin and I went first. I knew that there was a nice little café just up the hill and I headed that way. Unfortunately I chose to leave the pharmacy as one of what I might call the characters of the town passed by. He was about fifty years old and as thin as a rake, bald as a coot and had a habit of going out shopping while dressed in a very short mini-skirt.

He had chosen to wear a very, very short yellow mini-skirt that day and I followed him as his thin hairy legs worked their way up the hill towards my café while his shopping basket swung with his stride. I slowed down to let him get well ahead, he slowed to look into a shop window. I tried to overtake him, he quickened his pace. In the end I had to walk with my eyes tightly shut. The view I would have seen would, I fear, have put me off my lunch altogether.

Jillian continued her interviews after lunch. The patients were all elderly people and many looked a little confused when they arrived as if they were not sure what was going to happen or what they were supposed to do. Without exception they looked pleased after having had their sessions and the chance to put questions to a pharmacist and get some good advice. Each of them thanked Jillian as they left. She was, I think, also pleased with the reviews so far.

'It's like detective work,' she enthused after the seventh patient had left. 'I feel a bit like Inspector Morse collecting facts and details then trying to work out what has happened. I like the attention to detail, it is quite fascinating. Why is this patient taking this medicine? Why does the patient think its not working? Why has the doctor added another drug? What can we do to make the patient's life a bit easier? Its all very interesting.'

Jillian had a few minutes to spare before her next patient was due to arrive and told me a story that she had recently read which illustrated just why it is so important for medication reviews to be performed regularly.

'This was an elderly man, about eighty-five I think. He went to have an MUR and the pharmacist made a list of his medication. The patient was taking a strong pain reliever for arthritis, metoclopramide tablets for nausea, two drugs to treat Parkinson's Disease and a sleeping tablet.

'Looking back through his medication history, the pharmacist noticed that for a long time the man had only been taking one medicine, a simple pain killer, paracetamol, to ease his arthritis. Then the patient had complained that his arthritis had flared up and said that he thought the paracetamol wasn't strong enough. Several months before the medicine review was done the paracetamol had been replaced with a more powerful pain killer. All the other items were much more recent additions to his list of medication.

'It took a bit of detective work but eventually that pharmacist was able to work out what had happened. When the paracetamol was replaced with a much stronger pain killer, the patient complained that it made him feel sick. To treat the nausea the doctor then prescribed metoclopramide.

'That helped but the patient made that classic mistake of thinking that if one tablet works alright then two or three would be twice or three times better. Soon he was taking too much, dangerously too much. For some reason the doctor didn't notice how many extra repeat prescriptions for the metoclopramide the patient was ordering and this went on for quite some time.'

'Too much of that wouldn't be good for him, would it?' Lynne had stopped work to listen.

'No,' Jennifer went on. 'A high dose of metoclopramide, especially with older patients, can lead to what we call extra-pyramidal side effects. Shakes and twitches, you know?' Lynne nodded. 'He continued to take a high dose for some time and went back to his doctor when he noticed these effects were starting. But rather than being diagnosed with an adverse drug reaction, the patient was diagnosed as having the start of Parkinson's Disease because of his shakes.

'He was given Sinemet at first then, when that didn't seem to help, selegiline was added. Both are drugs for the Parkinson's but his shakes went on. The doctor increased the dose but then the patient complained that he couldn't sleep so he was prescribed the sleeping tablet as well.

'The reviewer finally worked out that he was taking the sleeping tablet to counter the Parkinson's drug which had a side effect of insomnia. He was taking the Parkinson's drugs unnecessarily because his shakes were caused by him taking too much of the metoclopramide. That had been prescribed because of his apparent need for a strong pain killer.'

'What happened?' Lynne had stopped work altogether by now and we both listened in amazement.

'When the review got back to the doctor he stopped all the patient's medication and started again. It turned out that he didn't really need that strong a pain killer at all, the paracetamol was just fine. So he didn't need any of the other drugs either. Just the paracetamol with a small dose of codeine, they used co-codamol, for his arthritis. That's all he has to take now.'

Jillian's eighth and last patient of the day arrived just then and she collected up her papers and led the way into the consulting room. The patient, a heavily overweight woman of about fifty-five with noticeably nicotine stained fingers, dumped a pile of carrier bags on the floor by the dispensary counter and followed her with the words. 'This hadn't better take long, I'm in a hurry.'

Within what seemed like a matter of minutes she was out of the room again, picking up her bags and heading for the front door. I watched as she pushed her way through the customers and went outside. Then she stopped on the pavement to talk to another similarly sized woman. I saw her put down her bags and shook my head sadly as she took the proffered cigarette.

'I don't think I can count that as a proper MUR,' Jennifer had followed the patient out and stood between Lynne and me as we watched the duo light up outside. 'It was a complete waste of time. I really don't know why she said she'd come at all if she wasn't interested in taking part in the scheme. She wasn't willing to discuss her medication or even answer my questions.

'According to the record of what we dispense for her, I could see that she takes medicines for elevated blood pressure, high cholesterol, diabetes and asthma. She has quite a complicated list of things to take and I had wanted to make sure she was taking all the drugs properly and getting the best out of her inhalers but she wouldn't tell me anything. She wasn't even willing to let me explain what we are trying to do.' We watched as the two women puffed large clouds of cigarette smoke into each other's faces.

'I had hoped to get her onto the smoking cessation scheme as well. That would benefit her in so many ways. Her asthma might improve, her blood pressure could come down, we could improve her cholesterol level, even the diabetes might benefit, her heart certainly would. She could lose some weight and take some exercise. She'd be a new woman in a few months time if she'd make time. But,' she sighed as she went to feed the wasted paperwork into the shredder, 'I can only do what she'll let me do.'

'Perhaps she'll come back when she's got more time,' I said, trying to encourage my colleague.

'Perhaps,' Jillian sighed again. 'Perhaps she will, perhaps she won't. I won't hold my breath.'

About fifteen minutes later Lynne nudged my elbow and directed my attention toward the pavement outside the shop. Jillian had gone to her office, taking the chance to sort out some other paperwork but her eighth and last patient of the day was still outside. She and her friend were blocking the pavement forcing passersby to step out into the road to get past them. She was gossiping and smoking with her friend as if she had all the time in the world. In health terms we both knew that she probably didn't have as much time as she thought she had.

25

I make no claim to success as a sportsman and am a rare spectator at sporting events. I will wrap up in several layers of clothing to watch one or another of my grandchildren play in a game of football, rugby or netball but otherwise I have little to do with sport. That cricket match I took part in with my dear old friend Pete Evans against the area manager near the outset of both of our careers was the last one I ever played in. At the risk of upsetting more than a few colleagues I will even support the theory that golf is a good walk ruined.

My lack of interest stems from childhood I suppose. I was the bespectacled beanpole hovering in the background when teams were chosen and I almost invariably ended up on the losing side. This happened to me regularly no matter what game we played. It might be football, cricket, rounders with the girls or cowboys and indians. The result was always the same. In adult life I have continued to resist getting involved with sports and games through a mixture of sheer laziness combined with lack of ability.

Incidentally I have always been puzzled by the definitions of games and sports. What is the difference? Is one played by teams rather than individuals? Is there sportsmanship when playing games? Or gamesmanship when involved with sport? Are the rules and regulations so very different between the two types?

Why do we talk about the sport of cricket yet have a game of it? Or a cricket match if it comes to that.

Apparently Ernest Hemingway was quoted as saying, "Only bullfighting, mountain climbing and auto racing are sports, The rest are merely games". Perhaps it comes down to how far one risks one's life but I still do not understand why such a fuss is made over either of them.

One aspect of sporting activity that further mystifies me is the concept of extreme sports. The definition of extreme in this case is somewhat vague but the general idea seems to be to compete against oneself rather than against another participant. To pit oneself against the elements as well as one's fears. To go further than you thought you could in order to gain an adrenaline rush even though such activities are often more than acceptably dangerous.

The term extreme sport seems to have been extended lately to include anything different from what the majority of people think is a sensible activity. While sitting on a ferry from Oban to Mull one day I met an otherwise apparently normal young woman who openly claimed to be addicted to what she called extreme knitting.

She told me that she carries her knitting wool and needles everywhere she goes and had knitted in, among other places, a tent pitched on a glacier in Greenland, while dog sledging in Norway and while resting on a ledge high on a Swiss mountain. Bobble hats, scarves and thick socks are understandably the usual result of all this extreme activity. She was wearing examples of each of them that day, all knitted in bright red wool.

Who am I, I thought as I listened to her tale as she told it on the windswept deck, to laugh at her efforts when the only comparable story I could tell was of extreme pharmacy. I tried to explain what I meant by extreme pharmacy but my words were lost among the screaming gulls and the sounding of the ship's siren as we docked at Craignure.

Extreme pharmacy should be easily defined. At first I thought it would be when one has to do something out of the ordinary like carrying on through the floods to provide a service, or coping with a flu pandemic or working amid the chaos of a store refit. Those activities might give you a buzz but they rarely require you to risk your life. Then I realised that the definition is much more worrying. Anyone who actually works in a pharmacy will recognise extreme pharmacy straightaway. It has become the way we work everyday.

Along with the new contract pharmacists have taken on a number of new roles. At the time I think those who greeted the changes believed that pharmacists were moving away from the dispensing part of the job to take on a more clinical role. At last, we thought, we would be freed from the repetition and routine of the dispensary and be able to make use of all the training and experience we have gained to help our patients.

We would run campaigns to promote health and healthy lifestyles such as smoking cessation and weight loss. We would provide tests for blood pressure, detecting diabetes, controlling cholesterol levels, checking INR, chlamydia and even, just lately, we have heard the suggestion that pharmacists could collect the biometric data required for passports and identification cards. We would spend our time reviewing patient's medication, ensuring they take their medicines safely and for the best effect. The list grows almost daily. It hasn't worked out quite as planned yet.

The main problem is that the new ideas and plans intended to reduce the dispensing part of our workload have not been introduced. All sorts of people, usually academics and administrators incidentally, pushed pharmacists into what they called 'a new age' without thinking for one moment how what they refer to as 'the people on the ground' would cope.

We needed to be able to delegate some of our responsibility to trained staff. While there are some accredited checking technicians coming through now, it is a slow and patchy process. The electronic transmission of prescriptions was supposed to ease our workload but it hasn't happened yet. Most of us are still waiting for the system to be up and working properly. The majority of companies either cannot or will not employ more staff to do the work. To do so, they say, would increase costs too much.

Then we were told that repeat dispensing systems were going to help us plan ahead but in many ways they just added to the paperwork. In fact adding to the paperwork has been the greatest change to our workload so far. Most pharmacists have ended up taking on the extra roles in addition to also dispensing an ever growing number of prescriptions.

One of the great changes that have occurred over the last forty years is the ownership of pharmacies. Most of them are now part of one of the big chains. Boots, Lloydspharmacy, Rowlands, Tesco, Sainsbury, Asda, Morrisons, Superdrug and various co-operatives make up the vast majority of the pharmacies in your neighbourhood. Other pharmacies may be run as franchises or in family groups. Only a relative few are still one man or woman operations.

The majority of practicing pharmacists therefore are employees of these large chains or work as freelance locum pharmacists, mainly for these few companies. I have worked for all of these large chains except Superdrug. There isn't one in my area. As there are very few pharmacists involved in the day to day running of these huge companies our influence at head office is slight.

Therefore the business methods are influenced by the need to make big profits for the shareholders rather than the needs of your local dispensary. Financial controls rule the day. Company-speak covers head office while leaving the 'people on the ground' exposed to the pressure.

One of the biggest costs of running any business is that of staff salaries. The easiest way to reduce your costs is to cut the number of your staff. Obviously therefore one of the greatest pressures on pharmacists and other managers is the need imposed by head office to reduce staff costs as much as possible. The result of this policy is a demand to employ fewer staff and sometimes less experienced or trained staff who won't cost as much.

Although the quality of dispensing training available nowadays has never been better, such is the pressure in the workplace that it becomes more and more difficult to retain people let alone replace experienced, competent pharmacy staff as the years go by.

So companies want cheap staff but on the other hand the companies want to make as much money as possible as well. The dispensing contract I mentioned earlier when coupled with the National Health Service's efforts to cut the cost of dispensing medicines has reduced the amount of income for pharmacies.

To make more money for their companies, pharmacists and their staff have to take on more of the new roles. The pressure from head office to perform more and more of these jobs and claim the maximum funding available gets greater by the day. It is not uncommon for middle managers to threaten pharmacists with lost pay rises or withheld bonuses if they don't find a way of claiming the full amount of these funds. Archie's warning about well-trained chimpanzees existing on ever fewer bananas was almost right but I don't think even he imagined the crushing pressure of the workload heaped on these hard working people as well.

Certainly those who take part in extreme sports risk serious injury if not their lives for a moment or two of ecstasy. However as extreme pharmacy becomes the norm in most companies the adrenaline rush is fading fast and the lives at risk are those of our patients. As I've often asked myself, why on earth do we do it?

Over the years I had made a little blacklist of those pharmacies that were simply too extreme for my peace of mind. There were just a handful of pharmacies on my list and they were there usually because the working practices were too casual or risky, or the manager's attitude was not to my liking or the area managers seemed a little too much like the bullying abusive types I thought I'd left behind in the old days.

One day I heard that one of those blacklisted ones had changed hands. It now belonged to one of the large chains. I hadn't worked for them very often and wasn't completely familiar with their ways but I hoped they would have made that pharmacy a more professional place to work. When I was booked to work there one day I had the opportunity to find out what changes had been made.

The pharmacy is only about six miles from my home so I had a gentle start to my day. It took just a little over ten minutes to get from my front door to the pharmacy. As I drove into town I began to wonder if I'd been wrong to blacklist them, perhaps the company had changed for the better in the last few years, maybe the systems had been modernised and perhaps a more effective management brought in.

As a locum pharmacist I often need to drive thirty or forty miles before starting work and although the countryside around the Marches and into mid Wales is beautiful, the time spent travelling does add to the stress of the day. Then driving home when you are tired and perhaps through the wintry darkness can seem interminable.

A journey to work that takes only a few minutes and the possibility of working for a good employer sounded quite attractive as I drove down the lane between scented hedges and cow parsley covered verges. Perhaps I might try becoming an employee again.

A red kite swooped low over the bushes and landed briefly on the road ahead. I slowed to watch his elegant flight as he spotted me and took off. Red kites have made a great comeback in mid Wales in recent years and now are spreading their territories across the border into the Marches. Apparently they have nested just a few miles away from my home. Pete Evans would have been delighted. Thinking these thoughts as I drove made for a nice relaxing start to the day.

Many of the staff I had worked with previously had left the pharmacy by now. Some had married and had children, others had simply moved on when the new owners took over. One of the pharmacy assistants and the dispenser were old acquaintances.

I soon found that there was a shop manager now who was not a pharmacist and in fact they hadn't had a regular pharmacist in the branch for some time. A number of relief managers and freelance locums like me were employed there instead. Often they had a different one each day of the week which must have been hard work for the regular staff to cope with.

'You pharmacists all have your own funny little ways,' Dorothy the dispenser said. 'And some of them are very odd.' She shuddered and mentioned a pharmacist who took his dentures out to eat, or rather suck, crisps. He'd said it was to stop the bits getting stuck under his plate.

Like many pharmacists he felt unable to take a proper break for lunch so he had seated himself down in a corner of the dispensary to eat a sandwich and suck his crisps. Dorothy had to try and work on amid the slurping and slushing noises he made while doing so.

In retaliation I told her about the old pharmacist who used to wash off the toffee stuck to his false teeth under the taps in the dispensary sink. We agreed that both were equally disgusting.

I soon heard that quite a few pharmacists had arrived to work at the pharmacy since my last visit but then they all left soon afterwards. Indeed I was told that several of them had left the company altogether.

Most of them had moved into the same line of work as me and become locum pharmacists. Some of them simply refused to work for this company ever again. As a self employed freelance pharmacist there is no-one other than oneself and the Royal Pharmaceutical Society to answer to. I asked why so many pharmacists had left the company in recent months.

'I suppose they got fed up with the way they were treated.' Dorothy told me and my heart sank.

*

The day started with a rush and Dorothy didn't have time to tell me what had happened to all those other pharmacists. Like most pharmacies this one dispenses methadone and other drugs on a daily basis to drug abusers. The majority of these patients in this area have become addicted to injected heroin although some have used crack cocaine and other substances.

If such a patient wants help to get off the drug a local drug advisory agency arranges for their nearest pharmacy to dispense a set amount of methadone or similar drug each day. Special prescriptions are written to allow us to give supplies in instalments rather than one large supply as the patients usually can't be trusted not to sell the drugs on or they might even take an overdose.

This service seems to be more attractive to a group of people who are traditionally vulnerable and hard to reach than having to attend a hospital or doctor's surgery. The aim is to reduce drug related harm particularly HIV, Hepatitis C and various bacterial infections picked up by their lifestyle. We hope they will take the methadone instead of their usual drug and eventually reduce the dose until they are not taking anything harmful at all.

The service we provide is a bit like the way people use nicotine replacement patches to stop smoking but it is even more difficult to achieve success. It takes a long time for many of the drug abusers to reach that stage. Some of them never do. Most of these patients are young people and the majority are quite polite and cause no trouble. There are however some exceptions.

Our second patient that day came in to collect her dose of methadone. I could hear her coming as soon as she walked through the door. She was a particularly unpleasant young woman who, I was told later, had been caught shoplifting on several occasions and warned that she would be banned from the place if she didn't behave herself.

She came into the shop shouting abuse at the staff and to top it all on this morning vomited all over a display of cosmetics. One of the pharmacy assistants helped me to carry the display out into the back yard where we threw buckets of water over it.

'I'll make a list of it later,' she said. 'We'll probably have to write it all off.'

I returned to the dispensary with the stench of her vomit everywhere. Other customers and patients had formed a queue by now so while one of the girls cleaned up, we set about serving them. Then the shop manager walked into the dispensary. She was not a pharmacist. She was new to her job having previously worked in an office somewhere. Her first remark to me proved that she had little or no idea of the work we performed.

'I want Dorothy to come and change a window display for special offers,' she whined.

'She can't,' I said in surprise that she should even ask. 'She's busy in here,' I added, then. 'Perhaps if there is no-one else to do it you could do it yourself.'

Later in the morning when we were getting really busy she wandered back into the dispensary to interrupt us again. Leaning casually on the work bench and so standing in the way she started chatting.

'They tell me you used to be the manager of a pharmacy round here,' she said. 'Can you give me any tips on how I could do the job?'

'Yes. Leave and get another one,' I snarled. Dorothy coughed in the background to hide her gasp. Now I know that you might think that I may have been a little less than patient with her but the day was going downhill fast. And then the phone started ringing.

'Who's that!' a voice shouted into my ear.

'My name is Rodgers, Paul Rodgers. I am the locum pharmacist here today.'

'Huh! I don't know the name. Who else is there?'

'A dispenser, a couple of assistants and a store manager. Can anyone of us help you?'

'Put the dispenser on!' I put the phone on hold and turned to Dorothy.

'I'm sorry,'I said. 'There's a nasty piece of work on the phone who wants to talk to you. Would you rather I dealt with him?'

'I can hear him,' Dorothy said. 'It sounds like our beloved group manager. I'd better see what he wants.'

We could all hear what he wanted. Dorothy was being blamed for the fact that some paperwork hadn't been done and he wanted it done straightaway.

'I'm sorry,' she was saying. 'I didn't know about that. We haven't had a regular pharmacist here for some time now and not all of the locums know enough about the companies systems to do it.'

He wasn't listening but continued to shout at the poor girl. I was dealing with one of the patients out on the counter but I could see Dorothy was close to tears. I had just decided to take the phone off her and try to placate him when there was one last shout, almost a scream, and he was gone. Dorothy replaced the receiver with a shaking hand.

'He's coming in later and wants to see that paperwork done,' she sniffed. 'I'm not sure how to do it. Do you know?'

In between dispensing and serving our customers and everything else that had to be done we found the relevant piece of paper and filled it in. Dorothy looked relieved and put the form carefully to one side.

'Is he always like that?' I asked.

'Yes,' Dorothy gritted her teeth. 'And worse. He's the main reason none of the pharmacists stay here for very long. We are short of staff but he won't let us have any more. If I was on my day off you'd have to struggle on by yourself. He wouldn't care.

'Someone calculated that we should have at least two more people here just to cover the present workload. We reckon he's on a big bonus if he can force down our costs. He carries on in the same way in all the branches in the area he covers.'

'I wonder why no-one has complained about him.'

'They have. Several people have. Head office don't seem to believe us. Sooner or later someone will thump him. I hope I'm there to see it.'

I have to admit that in a strange way I was curious to meet this character. Why was he ever appointed to his job? How did he get away with this bullying and abuse? Why hasn't he been sacked by now? Why hasn't anyone thumped him as Dorothy expected?

As the morning went on I quizzed Dorothy but she seemed reluctant to even think about him. She did tell me that he had described himself as a martinet, adding 'Whatever that is', and also mentioned that she had heard that despite being married he was carrying on with another also married pharmacist from a nearby town.

'Why doesn't someone just tell his wife?' I asked but Dorothy only shrugged.

'He could be right about the martinet though,' I added a few minutes later. Dorothy looked puzzled. 'He probably thinks it means someone who is a firm disciplinarian. It sometimes refers to those who impose an military-type discipline.'

'That'll be him alright,' Dorothy nodded.

'I bet he doesn't know that the definition can also include those who try to impose a tough discipline but are so ineffectual that they have to resort to bullying tactics to get anyone to follow them at all.'

'Yes, that's definitely him!' Dorothy smiled for the first time since the phone call.

*

It was just a little before lunch time when the 'martinet' arrived. He scowled at me as he walked in. Dorothy tried to introduce me to him but he ignored her and launched into a tirade about how hopeless all his staff were. He was nothing to do with me really, I was not employed by that company and therefore I had no business telling him what to do, but I began to feel quite uncomfortable in his presence.

He had been haranguing Dorothy for some time about Medical Use Reviews. These are usually known as MURs and are one of the extra services announced in that new dispensing contract by which pharmacists could claim a set fee from the National Health Service for undertaking this new clinical role. In practice of course while the individual pharmacists claimed the fee, the money was paid to the company. I was feeling really sorry for Dorothy by now and so took the liberty of breaking in.

'It isn't actually Dorothy's fault if no-one has done your MURs,' I said. He glared at me, his cheeks reddening, his lips pressed firmly together. At least that shut him up for a second. 'She can't do them herself and as you haven't got a regular pharmacist here you can't expect locums to do them all for you.

Especially if they have to work short staffed. We simply haven't got time. And we don't actually get paid for doing them. Your best bet would be to have a second pharmacist here for a few hours a week at least if you want to claim for doing the full number of MURs.'

'Is that so!' he turned back to Dorothy as a customer tapped on the counter behind me. I smiled and nodded to the customer to let her know I'd seen her. Arguing in front of the customers was something else that annoyed me and being abused in front of customers was something that no-one should have to tolerate. He had started shouting at Dorothy again but clearly included me in his comments.

'As you damned well know, we have to do four hundred MURs before the end of the year so we can claim the full funding from the NHS. You've only done one hundred and forty-seven at this branch. That's no way near enough. I want at least ten done today. And ten more tomorrow and ten every day.' He swung round to face me again, his nose inches from my face but I noticed he wouldn't look me directly in the eye. 'Any patient will do, it doesn't matter what drugs they're on. Just get the paperwork filled in properly and sent off. I expect you to do ten by four o'clock or else!' I turned away to serve the waiting customer. 'And don't walk away when I'm talking to you!'

'I have a patient to talk to,' I replied as calmly as possible. 'I'll deal with you in a minute.'

He raised his fist and I thought for a second that he was actually going to hit me. I'm not a fighting man at all. If trouble starts you would find me hovering in the background suggesting we put the kettle on and have a nice cup of tea. However, like all bullies he was also a coward at heart. He stamped out of the dispensary and slammed his way through the door out into the stockroom. It went very quiet. My customer spoke first.

'He's a miserable git,' she said.

'I'm sorry about all that,' I said. 'What can I do for you?'

'Well, I've got a bit of trouble with my heart, my blood pressure's haywire, my cholesterol level is over the top, and my kidneys, liver, lungs and brain have just about given up the ghost. Oh, and I've got a sore throat and a verruca.' She grinned at the puzzled look on my face. 'Only joking!,' she laughed. 'I've just come to collect my granddad's prescription. William Alfred Thornton, forty-four Meadow Drive, please.'

When our chirpy young friend had left I glanced at Dorothy. She was trying to concentrate on her work but still looked upset.

'I suppose I'd better go and see him,' I said. 'I'll be back in a minute.'

As I went out through the door I met one of the counter assistants coming the other way.

'He's gone,' she said. 'I've just seen him get into his car and go. Good riddance!'

We had just about got through the day with our nerves intact but as I said to Dorothy, 'What a way to have to work.' The poor girl looked shattered as we locked up and went home. It was easier for me of course, I wouldn't be working in that pharmacy again tomorrow, or ever if it comes to that, but she knew that she would be there day after day and would get the same treatment all over again.

I gave her my phone number in case she wanted my help anytime and suggested she started gathering evidence from her colleagues in case they ever needed to take him to a tribunal of some sort. I did hear some time later that following complaints from several pharmacists and other staff, the self-styled martinet had eventually been moved to another area. I wonder why they didn't sack him altogether?

*

Since leaving my job in the old company all those years ago to work as a locum pharmacist I had rather lost contact with their working methods. Once in a while I was asked to work in one or another of their branches. This usually only happened when one of their own relief managers was unavailable, perhaps taken ill or because of some other emergency.

In truth I didn't enjoy these days, they brought back memories of awkward systems and the bullyboy tactics of those aspiring middle managers in the 1980s many of whom were promoted way beyond their abilities. To make my impression of them worse I also found the company had become very slow to pay me for my efforts. By and large I enjoy my job but I don't do it for nothing. I have a family and bank manager to support just like everyone else. On the other hand however the occasional day working for the company gave me a chance to catch up with some old friends.

Then I was asked to work in one of their branches in a small town in mid Wales. I arrived to find that only one other member of staff and a part time dispenser had been planned in to work with me. We had a difficult day. It wasn't that anyone was missing, the company just hadn't planned for any more help.

A local agricultural show was taking place on the edge of town so the streets were busier than normal with lots of visitors. The dispenser had been ill, she wasn't really up to working flat out and went home early. Just the two of us struggled on.

Lunchtime came and I closed the pharmacy altogether. My young colleague was a bit worried about that but there was no way either of us could cope alone. We survived the day and I wrote a letter of complaint to the pharmacy superintendent responsible for the way they run their pharmacies when I got home. I told them about the situation which I believed constituted working in conditions dangerous to their patients, not to mention the unreasonable stress put on their staff.

Some time later I received a very bland letter from one of the pharmacy superintendent's minions at their head office saying that they 'regretted my poor experience' but I have since heard that they have done nothing to improve the situation.

During the drive back to my house after that 'poor experience' I resolved that I would not take any bookings from that company again but as it happened there was to be one more job for me to do for them. It was one of those very last minute bookings. In spite of my resolve I have always disliked saying no whenever I was asked to work for someone. It comes from being self-employed, I reckon. You just don't like to turn down a day's pay. To do so seems unlucky somehow.

*

I thought I had a day off until I picked up the phone at home at about nine o'clock on a calm summer evening.

'Is that you Paul? Paul Rodgers?' It was a voice I didn't recognise.

'Yes,'

'Oh good. I'm David Price, the manager at the pharmacy in Barnsgrove. I understand you're a locum pharmacist. One of my colleagues recommended you to me.'

'Yes I am a locum. Do you want to book one for a day? I have a few spare days available in my diary.' I was reaching for my diary as I spoke. I could easily tell him I was already working if I didn't want the job but I didn't like to say no straight off.

'Can you come tomorrow? It's late notice I know, a bit of an emergency. I've been trying to find an available locum all afternoon. My area office weren't very helpful but they said if I could find one myself it was alright. I'll see you get paid don't worry.'

'Yes,' I answered in spite of my earlier resolution to have nothing to do with that company. 'Tomorrow is fine.'

'Oh thanks!' he sounded so relieved. I wondered what the panic was all about, he sounded very worried but after a short pause and before I could ask, he went on. 'There's just one thing. I'm sorry to trouble you but I've got a bit of a problem at work tomorrow as well.' My heart sank. What have I let myself in for now?

'It isn't a problem with the pharmacy,' he said quickly, reading my mind. 'Everything is up to date, I think. All the staff should be in. They're a good bunch. I've got a dispenser and a trainee at the moment so you should have a straightforward day.'

'That'll make a change,' I replied. 'So what's the problem?'

'We are having a new pharmacy graduate here for the next twelve months and she's due to start tomorrow. Could you just have time for a chat to welcome her, show her round and keep an eye on her for me. Maggie, my dispenser will help to look after her as well and I'll be back the day after tomorrow. We don't know much about her. I haven't actually met her before but I'm told she's a good 'un. Could you do that for me?'

'No problem.'

*

The alarm clock went off at six-thirty as usual and soon I was up and ready to go to work. I had known as I took the booking that it meant a drive over to the very first pharmacy I had ever worked in forty years ago. Since finishing my training there I had, over the years, only occasionally visited Barnsgrove. With each time I called in I felt less and less connected to the place.

I knew that all the staff I remembered had gone. I had heard that Archie retired to live in a bungalow in the West Country and he had apparently taken up bird watching. His wife was still chasing foxes and shooting squirrels. He had threatened to write a book about his career but as far as I knew he hadn't.

Incidentally I've lost count of the number of retiring pharmacists who've said, 'there's a book in all this and I'm going to write it when I retire', but none of them has delivered one yet. That's one reason why I've written this account. Someone had to do it.

Mrs Moore had retired as well, as had her husband. Amy had moved on a long time ago and my old mate, Janet, had disappeared altogether to another part of the country. I didn't expect Barnsgrove pharmacy to feel any different from any of the almost one hundred others I had worked in since that first day.

The drive through the Worcestershire countryside that morning was very pleasant. It was a lovely day, there was a blue sky and puffy clouds overhead, the traffic moved freely and I sang along to the music on my radio. Soon I was passing the hair dressing salon above which I'd lived in my perm-scented flat and parked my car in the very spot where I'd kept my old van in 1968.

I went in to find that the shop had had a refit since my last visit. It all looked very smart and clean. And it was nice and tidy in the dispensary as well. A slightly nervous-looking young woman waited by the counter. She was dressed in a smart business suit and stood quite still with her hands clasped behind her back but her eyes were flicking everywhere. Trying to get her bearings, I thought to myself. I do that every time I walk into a strange dispensary for the first time.

'Hello I'm Paul,' I said. 'Paul Rodgers, your locum for the day.'

'Hi,' she smiled. 'I'm Sam Walker. I've just graduated this summer and I'm going to do my pre-registration year here. This is my first day.'

I introduced myself to the other staff and as they seemed to be quite capable of getting on with their work I suggested that Sam and I go up to the office for the welcome chat. She nodded and said that she'd been told that the manager was away and that I would be here to greet her.

The shop itself may have been given a smart refit but as we went through the door into the staff area and stockrooms I could see that little else had changed. I had a strange feeling of coming home. The brown and cream paint had gone it was true, replaced by blue and cream instead. I glanced at the door which I knew led down into the cellar and remembered the taste of Amy's soft kiss. We walked on past a row of new lockers standing near the foot of the stairs.

I led the way up to the manager's office and we entered a very stuffy room. It was only just after nine o'clock and it was very hot in there already as the sun beat through the dusty windows. A fan stood on the desk so I switched it on.

The large wooden desk looked familiar. It was the very same one that had once been covered with Archie's trays of paperwork, his bits and bobs of office equipment and, if I remembered my first day rightly, an apple and a mug of cold tea. Now there was a computer and one of those combined telephone-fax-photocopier machines in their place.

A large safe stood in the corner, a newer one now, and the shelves were still covered in files and boxes of paperwork. I even thought I could detect the aroma of herbal sweets. I wondered if the smell could be ingrained into the walls even after all these years. Maybe there would still be a tin of them in one of the drawers of the table. Or maybe it was just my memory playing tricks, associating a place with a particular smell. I'll check that later, I thought.

'Take a seat,' I said.

As I moved round the desk to the other chair I noticed a calendar on the wall. The picture for this month was a panoramic shot of Poole Harbour in Dorset. There were yachts sailing across the sparkling harbour, seabirds flying overhead and crowds of holiday makers were enjoying the lovely weather. Almost every day on the calendar had a note or reminder scribbled across it and on the current day the note said "new student". I pointed to the note as I sat down.

'That'll be you then.' I said. She smiled and nodded.

'The first day of my career out in the real world,' she murmured almost to herself then smiled and added more audibly as her eyes met mine. 'I wonder what the future will bring.'

I leaned back in the creaking chair, took a deep breath and then sighed at the memory of my first day in Barnsgrove forty years before. My own first impressions, thoughts and fears mingled in some mysterious way in my head with the way that Archie had welcomed me and with everything that had happened to me since that day.

'Well,' I began ...

Printed in Great Britain
by Amazon